The Health Care Worker's Primer on Professionalism

The Health Care Worker's Primer on Professionalism

SHERRY MAKELY, Ph.D., RT-R

BRADY PRENTICE HALL, UPPER SADDLE RIVER, NEW JERSEY 07458

12/2001

Library of Congress Cataloging–in–Publication Data

Makely, Sherry.
    The health care worker's primer on professionalism / Sherry Makely.
       p.   cm.
    Includes bibliographical references and index.
    ISBN 0-8359-5483-8
    1. Medical personnel Professional ethics. 2. Medical care—
Quality control. I. Title.
    [DNLM: 1. Health Occupations. 2. Interprofessional Relations.
    3. Ethics, Professional. 4. Career Mobility.   W 21 M235h 2000]
    R725.5.M35   2000
    610.69—dc21
    DNLM/DLC   99–17379
    for Library of Congress   CIP

Publisher: *Julie Alexander*
Acquisitions editor: *Barbara Krawiec*
Editorial assistant: *Stephanie Camangian*
Director of production and manufacturing: *Bruce Johnson*
Managing production editor: *Patrick Walsh*
Senior production manager: *Ilene Sanford*
Production liaison: *Julie Boddorf*
Production editor: *Karen Fortgang, bookworks*
Creative director: *Marianne Frasco*
Interior design: *Karen Fortgang, bookworks*
Cover design: *Bruce Kenselaar*
Marketing manager: *Tiffany Price*
Marketing coordinator: *Cindy Frederick*
Composition: *BookMasters, Inc.*
Printing and binding: *R. R. Donnelley, Harrisonburg, VA*

Printed in the United States of America

10 9 8 7 6 5 4 3 2 1

ISBN 0-8359-5483-8

PRENTICE-HALL INTERNATIONAL (UK) LIMITED, *London*
PRENTICE-HALL OF AUSTRALIA PTY. LIMITED, *Sydney*
PRENTICE-HALL CANADA INC., *Toronto*
PRENTICE-HALL HISPANOAMERICANA, S.A., *Mexico*
PRENTICE-HALL OF INDIA PRIVATE LIMITED, *New Delhi*
PRENTICE-HALL OF JAPAN, INC., *Tokyo*
PEARSON EDUCATION ASIA PTE. LTD., *Singapore*
EDITORA PRENTICE-HALL DO BRASIL, LTDA., *Rio de Janeiro*

Contents

Preface

WHO THIS BOOK IS FOR AND WHY IT'S IMPORTANT

The Health Care Worker's Primer on Professionalism is designed for students preparing for careers in health care as well as for new and current health care workers who could benefit from additional professionalism training. Information contained in this book applies to all types of health care workers including clinical staff (such as nursing and allied health personnel), clerical staff (such as secretaries, billing clerks, and insurance processors), and support staff (such as housekeepers, food service workers, and customer service representatives). Information also applies to workers in all types of settings where health care services are provided, including hospitals, clinics and other outpatient facilities, physician practices, home care agencies, long-term care facilities, public health organizations, schools, urgent care centers, and insurance and billing companies.

The information presented in this book is vital to the success of today's health care workers. Hands-on technical skills remain a high priority, but good character, a strong work ethic, and personal and professional traits and behaviors are becoming more important than ever before. Statistics indicate a growing concern with theft, fraud, and behavioral problems in the workplace. Poor attendance, interpersonal conflicts, disregard for quality, and disrespect for authority all too often lead to employees being fired from their jobs. With growing emphasis on customer service, cultural diversity, and corporate compliance, health care employers increasingly seek workers with strong "soft skills"—people who communicate appropriately, work well on teams, respect and value differences, and interact effectively with coworkers, patients, visitors, and guests.

Regardless of job title or discipline, every health care student and worker must understand the importance of professionalism and the need to perform in a professional, ethical, legal, and competent manner. Developing and strengthening professional traits and behaviors have become a major challenge for both health care educators and employers. *The Health Care Worker's Primer on Professionalism* helps meet that challenge. It describes professional standards that apply to *all* health care workers—the "common ground" that everyone shares in providing the highest quality of health care services for patients.

WHAT THIS BOOK COVERS

The Health Care Worker's Primer on Professionalism discusses the following:

- Which jobs require professionalism
- Definitions and key elements of professionalism
- Why professionalism is important to patients, employers, and health care workers
- Making a commitment to your job (the "big picture" and where your role fits in, work ethic, attendance, accountability, quality of work, compliance, representing your employer)
- Who you are as a person and what you contribute in the workplace (character, values, reputation, integrity, judgment, trustworthiness, honesty, ethics, morals)
- Working with others (relationships, teamwork, diversity, respect, manners, communication skills, conflict resolution, customer service)
- Personal skills and how they impact success on the job (personal image and appearance, personal habits and grammar, professionalism after hours; managing time, personal finances, and stress; problem-solving and critical-thinking skills; managing change)
- Personal and professional growth and advancement (career planning, personal assessments, basic skills, exploring employment opportunities, résumés, interviewing)

In addition to chapter readings, the book provides a Glossary of Terms, Exercises, Self-Assessments, Individual Next-Step Action Plans, What If Scenarios, Review Questions, and references to Supplemental Learning Resources.

APPLICATIONS FOR THIS BOOK

There are at least three ways to use *The Health Care Worker's Primer on Professionalism:*

1. As the textbook for a classroom-based, instructor-led course (a separate course on professionalism or as part of another course, using the *Instructor's Guide*)
2. As the textbook for an independent study, instructor-facilitated course (a self-paced, learn-on-your-own approach using the *Independent Study Guide,* which is included in the *Instructor's Guide*)
3. As personal reading (a self-instruction resource that includes exercises, self-assessments, etc.)

The Health Care Worker's Primer on Professionalism is designed for *all* nursing, allied health, clerical, and support staff and may be used in:

1. Educational programs that prepare new health care workers in
   - High school HOE (Health Occupations Education) programs
   - Vocational-technical programs
   - Community college and university programs
   - Hospital-based programs
   - On-the-job training programs
2. Orientation sessions for new workers to
   - Communicate performance standards for professionalism
   - Reinforce corporate mission and values
   - Explore how employees represent the company they work for
   - Support corporate compliance training
   - Emphasize customer service expectations
3. Additional training and refresher courses for experienced health care workers
   - Skills strengthening and performance improvement training
   - Individual performance improvement plans
   - In-service sessions
   - Continuing education
   - Cross-training programs
   - Retraining programs

HOW TO USE THIS BOOK

As mentioned earlier, this book can be used as personal reading or as the text for a classroom-based course or as an independent study course.

For personal reading, read a chapter, review the Glossary of Terms, and then complete:

- Supplemental reading assignment, if provided for that chapter (optional)
- Supplemental video viewing assignment, if provided for that chapter (optional)
- Exercises
- Self-assessment
- Individual Next-Step Action Plans
- What If Scenarios
- Review Questions (compare your answers with those at the end of the book)

After completing one chapter, move on to the next chapter.

For classroom-based courses, use the *Instructor's Guide*. For independent study courses, use the *Independent Study Guide* included in the *Instructor's Guide*. Both are described later in this Preface.

THE COMPLETE SET: PROFESSIONALISM FOR HEALTH CARE WORKERS

This book is one of three items in the complete set:

- *The Health Care Worker's Primer on Professionalism* book
- "Focus on Professionalism" videotape
- *Instructor's Guide* and *Independent Study Guide*

The "Focus on Professionalism" videotape is a valuable supplemental learning resource designed for use in conjunction with the textbook. The video presents five different scenarios, each demonstrating both professional and unprofessional behaviors. Although the video features medical assistants working in a physician's office, the concepts are applied to all types of health care workers in a range of settings. Through the guidance of a narrator, each scenario is presented twice. Opening scenes demonstrate poor professionalism and follow-up scenes demonstrate good professionalism. The narrator identifies each trait or behavior and discusses the role of professionalism in each situation. Each of the five scenarios complements a chapter in the textbook as well as a section in the *Instructor's Guide*.

The *Instructor's Guide* provides an overview of how to use the textbook and other materials in the set for either an instructor-led, classroom-based course or for an instructor-facilitated, independent study course. The general guidelines provide:

- Overview of the structure and content of the *Instructor's Guide*
- Details on how to use the *Instructor's Guide* for either a classroom-based course or an independent study course
- Template for a five-chapter lesson plan that is easily modified for any schedule or time frame; the instructor/facilitator decides which topics to emphasize, which exercises and assignments students should complete
- Course description and course objectives
- Master plan listing the basic content of all five chapters of the course
- Overview of teaching/learning methods
- Overview of evaluation tools and methods for demonstrating mastery
- Guidelines for using Exercises, Self-Assessments, Individual Next-Step Action Plans, What If Scenarios, Review Questions, Experiential Learning Activities, and Discussion Topics
- Detailed written assignments for Experiential Learning Activities
- Course materials list (required and supplemental)
- Rationale and guidelines for using the Supplemental Learning Resources

In addition to general guidelines, the *Instructor's Guide* also provides the following for each chapter of the classroom-based course:

- Curriculum outline
- Lesson plan
- Objectives
- Discussion topics
- Pre-/posttest with answer key
- Recommended responses to the What if Scenarios
- Print masters for selected chapter items

In addition to general guidelines, the *Instructor's Guide* also provides the following for independent study courses:

- Role and responsibilities of the student
- Role and responsibilities of the facilitator

The *Independent Study Guide* portion of the *Instructor's Guide* is designed for individuals taking an independent study course rather than a classroom-based course. Used in conjunction with the book, the *Independent Study Guide* allows for a self-paced approach or one that conforms to more of a structured schedule as determined by the facilitator. It provides a detailed, self-contained course of study that can be easily modified by the course facilitator. This includes:

- Guidelines and instructions for how to use the *Independent Study Guide*
- Description of the learning methods used
- Description of how mastery is demonstrated and evaluated
- Course materials list (required and supplemental)
- Description of the role, responsibilities, and expectations of the student
- Course description and course objectives
- Master plan listing the basic content of all five chapters of the course
- Chapter objectives
- Chapter assignments
- Detailed written assignments for Experiential Learning Activities
- Checklists of things to complete before moving on to the next chapter
- Examination guidelines

SUPPLEMENTAL LEARNING RESOURCES

In addition to the three-item Professionalism set an optional supplemental learning resource is the book *It's a Jungle Out There! An Insider's Outlook on Jobs in Health Care,* by Dr. Sherry Makely and Lana Christian. This timely resource describes the latest trends and issues in health care—information with which all students and workers need to be familiar. It discusses why and how health care is changing and examines the impact of change on patients, workers, employers, jobs, and career opportunities. Topics include managed care, organizational restructuring, work redesign, and cross-training. The book also describes skills in demand among health care employers and various issues to consider in career planning. *The Health Care Worker's Primer on Professionalism,* the *Instructor's Guide,* and the *Independent Study Guide* include references to *It's a Jungle Out There! An Insider's Outlook on Jobs in Health Care* and optional reading assignments.

For readers who would like to know more about cross-training, another optional supplemental learning resource is the book *Multiskilled Health Care Workers: Issues and Approaches to Cross-Training,* also by Dr. Sherry Makely. Written for managers, educators, workers, and students, this book describes the evolution of cross-training and how multiskilled personnel provide team-based care in today's restructured health care organizations. Topics include skill combinations, team composition, and approaches to educating and employing multiskilled personnel.

Information on how to order *It's a Jungle Out There! An Insider's Outlook on Jobs in Health Care* and *Multiskilled Health Care Workers: Issues and Approaches to Cross-Training* is included at the end of this book in the Supplemental Learning Resources section.

In Summary

We hope you find *The Health Care Worker's Primer on Professionalism* and other related materials informative and helpful.

Introduction

RECOGNITION AS A HEALTH CARE PROFESSIONAL

There's no doubt about it. When you're sick or injured, or when a family member or friend needs health care, you want to be certain that you and your loved ones are cared for by professionals. Thinking back to the times when you've had a doctor's appointment, visited an outpatient clinic or emergency room, or been hospitalized for tests or treatments, you probably encountered many different types of health care workers. Although most of these workers performed their duties in a professional manner, you may have encountered a few who did not. We would like to think that everyone who works in health care functions as a professional, yet experience has shown that such is not always the case.

What is a professional? How can you recognize a professional when you see one? What does "taking a professional approach" to one's work mean? Why is professionalism important? How can *you* be recognized as a health care professional yourself?

According to *Webster's New World Dictionary of the American Language, College Edition,* a professional is a person "with much experience and great skill in a specified role" who is "engaged in a specific occupation for pay or as a means of livelihood." As we look around us, we see many examples of professionals in different walks of life. In sports, for example, professional status is awarded to gifted athletes who have surpassed amateur events and moved into high-paying, major league competitions. In medicine, law, and science, people like doctors, lawyers, and engineers are considered professionals because of their expertise, college education, and special credentials like licenses and certifications. But truck drivers, hair stylists, and photographers consider themselves as professionals too, as do bankers, insurance underwriters, and investment counselors. Exactly what *is* a professional and who is qualified to be one?

Occupations are sometimes divided into "professional" and "nonprofessional" categories based on criteria such as:

- Unique and exclusive scope of practice
- Minimum educational standards and accreditation of educational programs
- Minimum standards for entry into practice
- Required credentials such as licenses or certifications
- Professional associations with codes of ethics and competency standards

When we apply these criteria to the health care workforce, doctors, registered nurses, pharmacists, physical therapists, medical assistants, surgical technologists, radiographers, and the like are all classified as professionals. That leaves all the other types of people who work for health care organizations in the nonprofessional classification, including secretaries, insurance claims processors, food service workers, environmental services and maintenance personnel, admitting clerks, telephone operators, landscaping and grounds personnel, equipment repair technicians, laboratory assistants, and scores of other employees. Not making the list of professionals can be demeaning to people who work hard and make their jobs a top priority in their lives.

Does this mean that your job must meet the criteria listed above for you to be considered a health care professional? Not necessarily. Other important criteria need to be considered, too. In fact, in the everyday life of health care organizations throughout the country, it's really more important to differentiate between *professionals* and *unprofessionals*. Everyone who provides direct patient care or who works in a supportive role is eligible for, and should strive for, recognition as a professional. For starters, professional recognition isn't something that's automatically bestowed upon a person when he or she completes a training program, obtains a college degree, or secures a license to practice. It's not dependent on a person's socioeconomic status, income, age, gender, race, job title, or position within the hierarchy of an organization. After all, we've all known people with college degrees, special credentials, and impressive job titles who don't behave in a professional manner.

Recognition as a health care professional is something that has to be earned— a reputation that's developed and maintained each and every day you come to work. Professionalism is a state of mind, a way of "being," "knowing," and "doing" that sets you apart from others. It gives direction to how you look, behave, think, and act. It brings together who you are as a person, what you value, how you treat other people, what you contribute in the workplace, and how seriously you take your job. Professionals don't just work to earn a paycheck. Income is important, but professionals view their work as a source of pride and a reflection of the role they play in society.

If you're serious about a career in health care, viewing yourself as a professional and being recognized as such by other people will be a major key to your success. Professionalism is something every organization looks for in its employees. How can you spot a health care professional when you see one? It's easy.

Health care professionals are good at what they do—and they like doing it. They enjoy helping others and knowing they've made a difference. Professionals have their personal "act" together—and it shows. They set high standards for their performance and achieve them. They see the "big picture" in health care and know where they fit in. Professionals care about quality and how to improve it. They treat everyone they meet with dignity and respect. And they continually strive to grow and to learn.

Spotting a health care professional may be easy—but becoming one yourself is another matter. It's something you have to concentrate on every day—but it's worth it.

In order to *be* a professional, you must *feel like* a professional. In our society, the amount of education a person has and what he or she does for a living have become important contributors to an individual's self-esteem and sense of self-worth. *What we do* has become *who we are*. If you have graduated from an educational program or earned a college degree, you've already experienced the exhilaration of knowing you've accomplished something worthwhile. If you haven't yet tackled postsecondary education or you don't plan to, excelling in your job can give you a sense of pride in knowing you've accomplished something important in life. Being recognized by others as a professional gives value and meaning to your efforts. It reminds you that what you do counts. This is true whether you perform patient procedures, process paperwork, prepare meals, clean public areas, order and stock supplies, or work in any one of hundreds of different health care jobs. No matter what your role involves, how you view your work and how you approach it can have a tremendous impact on your own life as well as on the lives of those you serve.

Why Health Care Needs Professionals

Health care is a basic need for survival. Each year, millions of Americans receive health services in doctor's offices, hospitals, outpatient clinics, long-term care facilities, and in their homes. Patients rely on health care professionals to provide affordable, state-of-the-art diagnostic and therapeutic procedures to help them overcome illness, injury, and other abnormalities that impact their health and quality of life.

But health care is a business too, and as consumers and taxpayers, we all pay for health services. Finding new ways to provide services for more patients, using fewer resources, while achieving higher-quality outcomes has become a major challenge for health care providers. The only way this challenge can be met is through a cadre of well-qualified employees committed to quality and cost effectiveness. People who fail to take a professional approach to their work are often absent, late, unreliable, and sloppy. Their actions may endanger quality of care, safety, and the appropriate use of limited resources.

Working in health care requires special skills and an attitude that supports service to others. Patients seek out health care services during some of the most vulnerable times in their lives, when they're sick, injured, and "at their worst." Each patient-worker interaction must build confidence and trust. The decisions and actions of people who care for patients, or whose work behind the scenes supports the efforts of caregivers, can have an immediate and lasting affect.

THE IMPORTANCE OF EVERY JOB AND EVERY WORKER

No matter what job you have, you play an important role in health care. No job is insignificant and no worker is unimportant. Regardless of how others may classify your job as "professional" or "nonprofessional," it's what *you* contribute that really matters. W*hat* you do and *how* you do it are extremely important, whether you provide hands-on care or function in a support role behind the scenes. Your challenge is to pull together the mixture of knowledge, skills, compassion, and commitment required to make you the very best employee you can possibly be. If you can meet this challenge and carry it through on a daily basis, then you've earned the privilege of being recognized as a health care professional.

No less is acceptable.

The Health Care Worker's Primer on Professionalism can help you on your journey toward professional recognition. The basic elements of professionalism are discussed, along with the personal and professional traits you need to be successful in your job and in the future.

Every health care employee has the opportunity and the obligation to strive for professional recognition. Always remember, it's not *the job* you do that makes you a professional, it's *how you do it* that counts.

The Health Care Worker's Primer on Professionalism

Chapter One

Making a Commitment to Your Job

CHAPTER OBJECTIVES

Having completed this chapter, students will be able to:

- ✔ Discuss why professionalism is important in health care.
- ✔ Describe the factors involved in being recognized as a health care professional.
- ✔ Explain why every job and every worker is important.
- ✔ List which jobs require professionalism.
- ✔ Describe the role they play (or will play) and how it fits into the "big picture" in health care.
- ✔ Describe a strong "work ethic" and explain its importance.
- ✔ Discuss how attendance, punctuality, reliability, and accountability impact their recognition as a professional.
- ✔ Describe the role of professionalism in quality of work, compliance, and representing their employer.

The Jobs That Require Professionalism

As discussed in the Introduction, no job is insignificant and no worker is unimportant. Just think about it. Everyone knows the roles of doctors, nurses, pharmacists, and physical therapists, for example, are important. But patients and the general public may not be as familiar with the roles of other caregivers such as medical assistants, radiographers, EKG technicians, nuclear medicine technologists, occupational therapists, and sonographers, just to name a few. People who work in support roles, often behind the scenes, may be even less known to patients and the general public. This includes billing clerks, instrument technicians, biomedical engineers, financial analysts, research assistants, and the scores of other kinds of personnel whose roles are also vital in health care. Depending on how you add them up, there are several hundred different jobs in health care organizations. Large urban hospitals and medical centers employ so many different types of workers, they begin to resemble small towns.

If your job involves direct patient care, it should be obvious that professionalism is important. The same holds true with jobs where workers interact with visitors, guests, and **vendors.** Examples include customer service agents, telephone operators, purchasing agents, accounts payable clerks, insurance processors, and departmental secretaries. But what about the large percentage of health care workers who work in support roles behind the scenes? If they don't interact directly with patients, visitors, guests, or vendors, is professionalism really important in their jobs, too? Let's take a closer look.

What if environmental services workers (housekeepers) neglected to empty trash containers in public rest rooms for several days, miscalculated the dilution of an antiseptic cleaning fluid, or used the wrong wax on the floor of a busy hallway? What if laundry workers failed to wash a bundle of patient sheets and towels, used the wrong soap in the washing machines, or took scrubs home as gifts for friends? What if landscapers skipped mowing the grounds, introduced plants causing allergic flare-ups, or left hedge trimmers laying on the walkway into the building? What if maintenance workers ignored a plumbing problem, left a weak stairway railing unrepaired, or forgot to do preventative maintenance on a refrigeration unit? What if food service workers put the wrong items on a special-diet patient tray, neglected to wash their hands after a trip to the rest room, or spilled hot grease near an open flame in the kitchen? What if central service technicians packaged the wrong supplies, failed to replace outdated stock, or operated sterilizers at the wrong temperature? What if security officers failed to follow protocol for reporting a fire alarm or used passkeys to steal computers from the company?

It should be obvious that professionalism is vital in *every* job. Each job exists for a reason. If there weren't a need for a job and having the responsibilities of that job performed appropriately, the job wouldn't exist. So it only stands to reason that every job is important—and doing the job well requires a professional approach to one's work.

The Big Picture and Where You Fit In

No matter what your job may entail, perspective is important. You must be able to step back and view "the big picture" to see where your role fits in. As a health care worker, you are part of one of the nation's largest and fastest growing industries. How much do you know about the industry in which you work? Are you up-to-speed on the latest trends and issues in health care? Do you have a national perspective on America's health care system—its history, current status, and where it seems to be headed? Do you know enough about the health care scene in your own part of the country to discuss how local issues compare with national trends?

Because you work in health care, other people who don't may look to you for information or advice. Because we are all consumers and taxpaying supporters of health care, most everyone has an opinion to share or a concern to discuss. People may ask you questions such as:

"What is managed care?"

"What's an HMO?"

"Why can't I go to any doctor I want to anymore?"

"What's a primary care physician?"

"Why are the two hospitals in town merging together?"

"Why did our hospital let some of its staff go?"

"Where are the best job and career opportunities in health care?"

Can you answer questions like these? If you want to be viewed as a professional, you need to be aware of what's going on in your industry and be able to talk intelligently about it with other people. This doesn't mean that you have to be a walking encyclopedia on health care. But you should keep up with the latest trends and issues on both the local and national levels. Be on the lookout for information from a variety of sources. Read articles about health care in newspapers and magazines. Watch the news on television and look for special programs about health care. Attend in-service sessions at work and seminars on health care topics whenever you get the opportunity. Get involved with a professional association. Talk with people who are current on the latest information, and join in conversations to learn more yourself and to share what you already know with others.

An excellent source of information that you may wish to read is a book called *It's a Jungle Out There! An Insider's Outlook on Jobs in Health Care* (refer to the Supplemental Learning Resources section at the end of this book for ordering information). *It's a Jungle Out There! An Insider's Outlook on Jobs in Health Care* provides the latest information about the health care industry—how and why health care is changing; how these changes affect employers, employees, and patients; and what kinds of skills are in demand among employers. Not only will this information benefit you directly as a health care worker, but it will also provide the background knowledge you need to be well versed in your industry's trends and issues.

Equally important to having an awareness of the big picture is knowing where *you* fit into that picture—especially within your own organization. This begins by developing a **systems perspective**—standing back, viewing the entire process of how a patient moves through your organization, and seeing how your job fits into that process. No one in health care works in a vacuum. That is, everyone's work is interconnected. Only when your efforts are well coordinated with those of other employees can your company conduct its business and meet its goals.

Think about your job and your responsibilities. How do they connect with those of other workers? How does your role interface with the roles of other workers to carry out your company's business? What other workers must you depend upon to get your work done? What other workers depend upon you to get their work done? And where do the patients fit in?

From a systems perspective, ask yourself the question, "What could happen if *I* didn't take a professional approach to *my* work and get things done in an appropriate manner?" What if you failed to show up for work without notifying someone or arrived several minutes or hours late for your shift? What if you "dropped the ball" and didn't follow through on an assignment or job duty? What if you got sloppy and made a mistake? What if you weren't concentrating on what you were doing and missed something important? What if you showed up for work impaired by alcohol or some other drug? What if you ignored the rules or violated a policy or a law? What if you let your skills slip and didn't keep up on a new procedure or piece of equipment? What effect would an "I don't care" attitude have on your job performance?

What impact does your performance have on the organization you work for and on the patients it serves? Remember, if your job weren't important, it would not exist. So just how important *is* it? Professionals can answer that question easily because they see the big picture and know where they fit in. They know that other people are counting on them, and they can predict what might happen if they don't follow through.

If you don't perform your job well by meeting the expectations that management has set forth for your position, you won't be in that job for very long. You may be able to hide incompetence, sloppiness, and indifference for a while, but eventually poor performance will catch up with you. What's worse, someone (or several people) could be victimized by your lack of professionalism in the meantime. If any of the "what if's" listed above sound like they might apply to you and how you approach your work, make a conscientious decision right now to resign and get out of health care altogether, or make a promise to yourself to improve—and keep reading.

A Strong Work Ethic

Ask just about any type of employer what characteristic is most important in a good employee and the majority will respond, "A strong **work ethic.**" This means positioning your job as a high priority in your life and making sound decisions about how you approach your work. Employees with a strong work ethic stay focused and leave their personal problems at home. They apply themselves to the task at hand and take a thorough approach to getting the work done right—the first time. They exercise self-discipline and self-control. They know what management expects of them and they measure up. Not waiting to be told what to do, they demonstrate initiative, motivation, and enthusiasm for their work.

Let's examine some of the other factors involved in developing a strong work ethic and demonstrating a commitment to your job and to the organization that employs you.

Attendance and Punctuality

It's nearly impossible to demonstrate a commitment to your job without being there! Performing the duties of your job requires showing up for work every day and being **punctual.**

Poor attendance usually results in other people having to cover for you when you aren't there yourself. How does it make you feel when your coworkers call in sick frequently, leaving you to do your work plus theirs? How do you think *they* feel when *your* attendance leaves a lot to be desired? Many health care organizations are already lean on staffing and can't afford to have people absent on a regular basis. It's important to be there when people are counting on you—and to arrive on time.

When you arrive late for work, you hold things up and inconvenience other people. A patient's procedure might have to be rescheduled, possibly delaying someone's diagnosis, treatment, surgery, or discharge from the hospital. Needed supplies might not get delivered on time, paperwork might be filed too late to meet a deadline, or other people might have to work beyond their shifts to get caught up. Remember how the roles of health care workers are interconnected? You may think that arriving late for your own job is not a problem, but what kinds of complications are you causing other people?

Most everyone must miss work or arrive late on occasion. But when poor attendance or punctuality becomes a habit, it also becomes a performance issue and possible grounds for **corrective action** or **dismissal.**

Make a commitment to show up for work every day, to arrive on time, and to be ready to work when your shift starts. Have **contingency plans** to cover situations when your children or spouse gets sick or when your transportation is unreliable. Protect your health and safety to keep from getting sick or injured yourself. Eat well, make sure you get enough sleep, think about getting a flu shot, and avoid unnecessary risks that might injure you.

When you arrive at work, give yourself enough time to park your car or get from the bus stop to your work area a few minutes early. When your shift starts, be sure you're in the area and ready to go. It's always better to arrive a little early than a little late. Supervisors notice who shows up early and who's in place, ready to work when the shift begins.

Try to allow some extra time at the end of your shift in case you get held over. Never leave a patient, coworker, visitor, or guest "hanging" by rushing out the door the minute your shift ends. It's your responsibility to stay long enough to complete your work or to hand it off to the person who follows you. Make sure there's a smooth transition between shifts and don't leave your work for other people to finish up. As mentioned previously, your job is important or it wouldn't exist. People are counting on you to get your part of the work done.

Reliability and Accountability

Being **reliable** and **accountable** are key factors in professionalism. If someone agrees to help you and then doesn't follow through, how does that make you feel? If getting your work done on time depends upon other people getting their work done on time, what happens when someone drops the ball? From a systems perspective, each worker is responsible for completing the duties of his or her job appropriately so that other people can complete their work, too. Make sure you get your own work done on time so you don't hold other people up. If you've told someone he or she can count on you, prove you are a reliable person and follow through. If you're there for others when you say you will be, it's more likely that other people will be there for you when you need them. Following through on commitments is a big part of the team effort.

Accepting responsibility and the consequences of your actions is also important. Professionals hold themselves personally accountable and avoid shifting the blame to others. If you make a mistake (and everyone does occasionally), admit it and accept full responsibility. Remedy the situation, personally apologize to anyone who's been inconvenienced, learn from the experience, and avoid making the same mistake twice. Your supervisor, coworkers, and other people will appreciate your "the buck stops here" attitude.

Accept all work assignments, follow instructions, and meet your deadlines. Refusal to complete a task as assigned may be construed as **insubordination** and grounds for dismissal. If for any reason you object to an assignment because it conflicts with your religious beliefs, morals, or values, you must discuss these concerns with your supervisor. It's best to resolve issues like these when you first consider a job offer. If you wish to not participate in abortions, sex change operations, end-of-life procedures, or other such activities, many employers will allow you to opt out, but this must be discussed ahead of time so patient care is not delayed or jeopardized.

QUALITY OF WORK

No matter where your job falls within the organizational structure of your company, the quality of your work is extremely important. What does quality mean to you? What do you think quality means to your employer and to the patients you serve? How does your work support quality? What factors erode quality?

Quality requires **competence**—possessing the necessary knowledge and skills to perform your job appropriately and safely on a daily basis. Make sure you are well trained and competent to perform each and every function associated with your job. Never take a chance and just "wing" it. Although your supervisor will probably evaluate your competence and review your work performance periodically, it's up to you to keep your knowledge up-to-date and your skills sharp. Learn about the latest procedures, techniques and new equipment. Attend in-service sessions and continuing education workshops, and read publications in your field. Never hesitate to ask questions or request help. And remember, just because you've completed your training doesn't mean your education ends. Nothing stays stagnant in health care. You must always keep learning and striving for ways to improve the quality of your work. As a professional, it's your responsibility.

Perhaps you've heard the saying "Quality is in the details." This means making even the smallest error or overlooking even the most minute detail can have a negative impact on quality. This includes putting stock items on the wrong shelf, misfiling a patient's record, losing a telephone number, miscalculating a bill, forgetting to order next week's supplies, or missing an important meeting because you forgot to write it down. Each day there are thousands of opportunities for details to "fall through the cracks." Being **diligent** about quality can help prevent these kinds of problems.

Taking an *un*professional approach to your work can certainly damage quality. Being lazy or sloppy, not paying attention, working impaired, operating equipment without proper training, or ignoring safety precautions can all lead to serious outcomes. You could hurt yourself or someone else, damage expensive equipment, waste valuable resources, or put yourself and your employer legally at risk. Always pay attention to what you are doing and look for opportunities to improve the quality of your work.

It's also important to contribute to quality improvement company-wide. No one has a better handle on how to improve work processes and quality outcomes than the people who actually do the work on a daily basis. Management can't improve the company's quality without your help. When you have a suggestion for quality improvement, submit it to your supervisor. When you spot a potential problem area, report it.

Responding to a request by saying "That's not my job!" is unacceptable. Doing what's asked of you might not fall within your job description, but one of two things needs to happen. Either you should go ahead and perform the task because you're capable of doing it and willing, or you should refer the matter to the appropriate person and then make sure he or she follows through. No task is too menial when working in health care. If a patient or visitor becomes ill in the parking garage, stay there and offer assistance or send for help. If someone looks lost, ask if you can provide directions. If you notice a spill in a public hallway, don't wait for a housekeeper to discover it. Either clean it up yourself or report it to the appropriate person and then remain in the area until it's cleaned up to prevent any unnecessary injuries. If you observe that a piece of equipment is not working properly, or spot a situation that might pose a health or safety hazard to someone else, don't just go on about your business. Take action! A commitment to quality means paying attention to what's going on around you and addressing concerns before they escalate into serious problems.

COMPLIANCE

Compliance with company policies and federal and state laws is extremely important. Ignoring a rule, violating a policy, or breaking the law can compromise quality and get you fired from your job.

What might happen if employees don't wear their identification badges at work? What if they ignore infection control precautions or leave confidential reports laying out in the open? What if they falsify documents or make threats against other employees?

Rules and policies are established for good reasons, and it is your responsibility to follow them. Health care organizations usually have written policies and printed employee handbooks to communicate expectations. Know where to find these policies and, if you don't understand something, ask for clarification.

Corporate compliance is becoming an important topic in health care. Complying with federal and state laws and various internal and external policies and procedures has always been important. But compliance is gaining even more attention these days because the government is stepping up its efforts to identify violators and prosecute them. Hospitals and other health care organizations have begun creating new departments to oversee compliance issues. They're training employees to spot problems and report them. They're auditing individual departments to uncover and resolve any compliance concerns. Many companies are setting up hot lines so employees can make confidential phone calls to report compliance concerns anonymously with no fear of backlash.

Violating a law, regulation, or policy can get you and your employer in serious trouble. You could end up fired, prosecuted, fined, or incarcerated. Your employer could face stiff fines and exclusion from vital government programs like Medicare or Medicaid. Complying with laws, regulations, and policies because you have to is important, but there's more to it than that. Professionals comply because it's *the right thing to do.*

Make sure you're aware of, and understand, all of the laws, regulations, and policies that pertain to your job. Know where your organization stands on practicing sound business ethics and what is expected of you. If you're accused of an illegal activity and claim "I wasn't aware of that law!" not knowing is not an acceptable legal defense. It's your job to know what laws, regulations, and policies apply to you and your work. If you're uncertain about any of them or unsure as to your own responsibilities, be sure to ask for clarification.

Some areas of risk that result in compliance concerns include patient **confidentiality,** safety and environmental precautions, labor laws, retention of records, Medicare billing and reimbursement, licensing and credentials, and **conflict of interest.** Examples of illegal or unethical behaviors include fraudulent billing (charging a patient for a test or treatment that he or she never received or coding medical procedures inaccurately), improperly changing or destroying records, personally profiting from self-referrals or insider information, **sexual harassment,** creating a **hostile workplace,** stealing property, and other dishonest acts.

Consider each of these issues and how it might affect your job. For example, always maintain the confidentiality of patient records, financial reports, and other materials that your employer deems private. Observe all safety and environmental regulations. Never accept pay for hours you did not work. Do not modify or destroy patient or financial records without proper authority. If your job involves billing the government or insurance companies for patient procedures, make sure the codes you use to identify specific diagnoses or procedures are accurate. Never up-code a procedure to increase reimbursement. Avoid any suggestion of a conflict of interest. For example, if your job involves awarding contracts to outside companies, don't accept gifts or free meals from a vendor in exchange for awarding it your company's business. Don't ask a vendor that your company does business with to give you a special discount on a personal purchase, and don't refer patients to one of your relatives who just happens to be in the health care business!

Make sure you work within your **scope of practice.** Performing duties beyond what you're legally permitted to do is highly risky and may be illegal. Some jobs require a special **license** to practice. State agencies grant licenses only to people who have met preestablished qualifications, and only licensed workers may legally perform the job. Other jobs may require a special **certification.** State agencies and professional associations certify people who have met certain competency standards. Although noncertified people may legally perform the job, employers may prefer to hire only those workers who possess certification and who are eligible to use the professional title associated with that certification. When a license, certification, or some other special credential is required for your job, make sure you meet those requirements and maintain an active status over time.

Avoid any suggestion of unwelcome, sexually oriented advances or comments that could lead to sexual harassment charges being filed against you. Even if you think your actions or comments are harmless, the other person (or someone else present at the time) might see things differently.

Never bring a weapon to work and never create a hostile or uncomfortable work environment for someone else. Verbal threats, nasty letters or voice mail messages, or other forms of hostile behavior may lead to charges of intimidation.

As a professional, you would never knowingly engage in an illegal or unethical act yourself, but you might observe someone else doing something suspicious. Or you might feel you yourself are a victim of sexual harassment or a hostile work environment. If you have a concern about something you see going on at work that might put you, your employer, your coworkers, or your patients at risk, be sure to let your supervisor know or report your concern via a hot line if one is available. If your supervisor is one of the people involved in the activity, report the matter to your supervisor's boss, to a human resources representative, or to someone in legal services. If you feel you're the victim of sexual harassment or intimidation, report the incident immediately. It's wise to keep written documentation of what you've observed or experienced, including details such as the date, time, place, who else was present, and a description of what exactly happened and what you did to follow up. Information like this will be very important during an investigation.

Based on the law, if you know someone else is engaged in illegal behavior, it's your responsibility to report it. If you don't, you could get in trouble, too. In fact, even if you didn't know but *should have* known, you can be liable for legal action. For example, if you observe someone stealing from patients, report it immediately. If you don't report it and your supervisor finds out that you knew what was going on, you too could be disciplined. If your job involves maintaining an inventory of supplies and a coworker gets fired for stealing some of them, you could get in trouble too for not noticing that items were missing. Keep on your toes and stay alert! If you find yourself in a situation where you aren't sure how to proceed, ask yourself some questions. Is what's going on legal and ethical? Is it in the best interests of my employer and patients? How would this look to others outside my organization? Then take action.

You've probably heard the term **whistle blower**—a person who "blows the whistle" on another person or on a company involved in wrongdoing. Blowing the whistle can be a scary proposition for employees, but the law protects whistle blowers from retribution. In fact, whistle blowers might receive a portion of the fines the government collects from health care organizations found guilty of Medicare fraud, for example. If you suspect someone of illegal or unethical behavior, it's your responsibility to report it. It's best to try to get your concern resolved within your organization first. Avoid going to the government or to the media unless repeated attempts have failed. If you've tried your best to report and stop illegal or unethical practices but have been unsuccessful, you might need to think about finding another job.

REPRESENTING YOUR EMPLOYER

When you accept a job offer, show up for work, and receive a paycheck, you become a representative of your company. To patients, visitors, guests, and vendors, you *are* that company. Everything you do and say can have an impact on the company's reputation. By accepting employment, you not only agree to follow your company's rules and policies but also agree to support its mission and abide by its values. What is your employer's **corporate mission?** What are the company's **corporate values?** What do *you* do to support the mission and values?

Learn everything you can about your company so you can talk intelligently about it with others in the general public. Read company newsletters and keep up on the latest events. Even though you don't *own* the business, it's still *your* company, so take an interest in it. You're an important part of the company you work for, and you have an obligation to get involved and support your employer. This begins with the language you use. When referring to your employer, avoid words like *they* and *them*. Instead, use *we* and *us*. For example, instead of saying "They told us they will open the new clinic next week," it's better to say, "We're opening our new clinic next week." It's not *they* did something or *they* said that, it's *us* and *we*. Take some pride and "ownership" in the company you work for. It's part of being a professional.

Regardless of what job you have, your appearance, attitudes, and behaviors reflect the company you work for. **Front-line workers** such as nurses, housekeepers, phlebotomists, patient transporters, and food service workers have some of the greatest influence on the company's reputation because they have the most frequent contact with patients, visitors, and guests. What might happen if you openly criticize your employer or complain about a company policy in public, or if you question how a physician, nurse, or other caregiver treated a patient? By damaging the reputation of your employer, you're hurting yourself and countless other employees who come to work each day to do a good job. If you have complaints or concerns, there are appropriate ways to communicate them *inside* the organization. Don't make negative remarks about your company or its employees in public. Use **discretion** and be careful what you say and to whom you say it. Give your employer and your coworkers the benefit of the doubt and assume that everyone is there to do his or her best. If you have serious doubts about your employer and the way your company does business, it's probably best to find another job.

Understanding the importance of professionalism, knowing where you fit into the big picture in health care, demonstrating a strong work ethic, improving quality, complying with laws and policies, and representing the company you work for in a positive manner are all important aspects of being recognized as a professional. The next step is examining who you are *as a person,* to see how your personal values and character traits support professionalism in the workplace.

GLOSSARY OF TERMS

vendors   people who work for companies with which your company does business

systems perspective   stepping back to view an entire process to see how each component connects with the others

work ethic   attitudes and behaviors that support good work performance

punctual   arriving for work on time

corrective action   steps taken to overcome a job performance problem

dismissal   involuntary termination from a job or from an educational program

contingency plans   a backup plan in case the original plan doesn't work

reliable   can be counted upon; trustworthy

accountable   accepts responsibility and the consequences of one's actions

insubordination   refusal to complete an assigned task

competence   possessing necessary knowledge and skills

diligent   careful in one's work

corporate compliance   acting in accordance with laws and with a company's rules, policies, and procedures

confidentiality   maintaining the privacy of certain matters

conflict of interest   an inappropriate relationship between personal interests and official responsibilities

sexual harassment   unwelcome, sexually oriented advances or comments

hostile workplace   an uncomfortable or unsafe work environment

scope of practice   boundaries that determine what a worker may and may not do as part of his or her job

license   a credential from a state agency awarding legal permission to practice; must meet preestablished qualifications

certification   a credential from a state agency or a professional association awarding permission to use a special professional title; must meet preestablished competency standards

whistle blower   a person who exposes the illegal or unethical practices of another person or of a company

corporate mission   special duties, functions, or purposes of a company

corporate values   beliefs held in high esteem by a company

front-line workers   employees who have the most frequent contact with a company's customers

discretion   being careful about what one says and does

✍ EXERCISES

Complete the following.

1) List ten different types of jobs you can think of in hospitals and in other settings where health care is provided. Then indicate which of those jobs require a professional approach to one's work.

_____

_____

_____
_____
_____
_____

2) List the essential functions of your job or the job you expect to have after completing your training. Draw a diagram to demonstrate how your role fits into the big picture of health care in your organization, and indicate what other types of workers you must interact with to get your work completed appropriately.

_____
_____
_____
_____
_____
_____

3) Think about your job or the job you expect to have after completing your training. Write three scenarios of what would happen if:
   a) you knew you were going to be two hours late for work but forgot to call and notify someone.

_____
_____
_____
_____
_____
_____

   b) you weren't paying attention, made a mistake, and then blamed it on someone else.

_____
_____
_____
_____
_____
_____

   c) you promised to help a coworker with a project and then forgot about it.

_____
_____
_____
_____
_____
_____

4) Make a list of what you think are the Top Ten Ways to Get Fired.

_____
_____
_____
_____
_____
_____

5) List five examples of how you take a professional approach in your work.

_____
_____
_____
_____
_____
_____

6) List five strategies to help ensure good attendance and punctuality.

_____
_____
_____
_____
_____
_____

7) What are the corporate mission and corporate values of the organization you work for or the school you attend? Do you support the mission and values? If so, how? If not, why not?

_____
_____
_____
_____
_____
_____

8) List five ways you can take an interest in, and get involved in, the organization you work for or the school you attend.

_____
_____
_____
_____
_____
_____

9) Rewrite the following statement to better reflect how you represent your employer or your school:

Last week they called everyone into the conference room. They told us they were changing two of their policies and described what we had to do to comply.

_____

_____

_____

_____

_____

_____

✍ SELF-ASSESSMENT

Think about yourself and how you approach your work. Consider each of the following and check all that apply.

_____ **1)** I keep up on health care trends and issues and can discuss them intelligently with other people.

_____ **2)** I'm familiar with the essential functions of my job and I know how my role connects with the roles of other workers.

_____ **3)** My attendance is very good and I am rarely late.

_____ **4)** When my shift begins, I'm in the area and ready to start work.

_____ **5)** I have a backup plan in case my transportation falls through.

_____ **6)** When I tell someone I'll help him or her out, I always follow through.

_____ **7)** I watch for ways to improve quality and submit suggestions to my supervisor.

_____ **8)** If something needs to be done and I'm not qualified to do it, I find someone who is and make sure the task gets completed.

_____ **9)** I read my employee handbook and follow my company's rules and policies.

_____ **10)** I'm aware of the laws and regulations that relate to my job and always adhere to them.

_____ **11)** If I spot a potential safety hazard, I make sure it gets fixed before someone gets hurt.

_____ **12)** I would never violate the law, even if my supervisor told me to.

_____ **13)** I maintain the confidentiality of all patient information and other matters deemed private by my employer.

_____ **14)** If my job requires a license or certification, I meet all requirements and maintain an active status.

_____ 15) I'm familiar with the scope of practice of my job and I refuse to perform procedures I'm not qualified to perform.

_____ 16) If I saw a coworker engaged in illegal or unethical behavior, I would report it to the appropriate person.

_____ 17) If I disagreed with a company policy, I would discuss it with my supervisor but not with the media or the general public.

_____ 18) If someone asked me to falsify a financial record, I would refuse to do so and then report it.

_____ 19) I know my company's corporate mission and values and do my best to support them.

_____ 20) I know my job is important and I always strive to perform it in a professional manner.

_____ 21) I'm a reliable person and I hold myself personally accountable for my actions.

_____ 22) I keep my skills up-to-date and I'm always learning something new.

INDIVIDUAL NEXT-STEP ACTION PLANS

Based on your Self-Assessment, complete the following.

1) My strongest skills are:

_____

_____

_____

_____

_____

_____

_____

2) My areas for improvement are:

_____

_____

_____

_____

_____

_____

_____

3) Five things I plan to do to improve my skills:
   a) _____
   b) _____
   c) _____

    d) _____

    e) _____

✎ WHAT IF SCENARIOS

What would you do in the following situations?

1) You were out with friends until very late last night and had to report for work this morning at 7:30 A.M. You know your coworkers won't arrive for another half hour, and you've got just enough time for a quick nap on a patient cart that's kept in the supply room.

_____

_____

_____

_____

_____

_____

2) You promised your coworkers you'd work the day shift on Thanksgiving so they could be home with their families. Then two days before the holiday, an old friend from out of town calls to say he'd like you to be his guest for lunch on Thanksgiving Day.

_____

_____

_____

_____

_____

_____

3) You car breaks down on Thursday night, and you have to be at work at 8 A.M. on Friday morning.

_____

_____

_____

_____

_____

4) You start your new job at 7 A.M. on Monday morning, but you have a habit of turning off your alarm clock and falling back to sleep without realizing it.

_____

_____

_____

_____

_____

_____

_____

5) Your shift ends in thirty minutes and you've got about thirty minutes of work left to do, but you haven't gotten to take your afternoon break yet.

_____

_____

_____

_____

_____

_____

6) Your supervisor asks you and two of your coworkers to proofread a financial report to make sure the calculations are accurate. Your coworkers have already reviewed the document and found no errors. You waited until the last minute to start reviewing the material and now it's time for you to go home.

_____

_____

_____

_____

_____

_____

7) You overhear a purchasing agent talking on the telephone with a salesperson from a local computer company. She offers to buy fifteen new computers for your company if the salesperson will also agree to sell her son a computer at the same quantity discount.

_____

_____

_____

_____

_____

_____

8) The office manager of the clinic where you work tells you to enter a code on an insurance claim form that she knows is not correct. If you enter the incorrect code that she tells you to, the clinic will receive more money from the insurance company than it would if you enter the correct code.

_____
_____
_____
_____
_____
_____
_____

9) You're a patient care assistant at a hospital and one of your neighbors is admitted to the unit where you work. A relative of yours calls to tell you he's heard a rumor that the neighbor has a communicable disease. Because you work on the unit and have access to records, your relative asks you to find out if the rumor is true.

_____
_____
_____
_____
_____
_____
_____

10) A new piece of equipment gets installed in your department, but you miss the in-service session when everyone was trained on how to operate it. The next day there's a procedure to be done using this equipment and it's your responsibility to do it.

_____
_____
_____
_____
_____
_____
_____

11) A coworker invites you to a party. When you arrive, you notice three other people that you work with complaining about low wages and telling a group of strangers that one of the surgeons at your hospital made a mistake in surgery last week and lied to the patient's family to try to cover it up.

_____
_____
_____

_____

_____

_____

_____

✍ REVIEW QUESTIONS

Answer each of the following.

1) Describe a health care "professional."

_____

_____

_____

_____

_____

_____

_____

2) What does it mean to take a professional approach to one's job?

_____

_____

_____

_____

_____

_____

_____

3) List ten jobs that require professionalism.

_____

_____

_____

_____

_____

_____

_____

4) Why is it important to be aware of trends in health care?

_____

_____

_____

_____

_____

_____

_____

5) Discuss what is meant by a systems perspective.

_____
_____
_____
_____
_____
_____
_____
_____

6) Define *corrective action.*

_____
_____
_____
_____
_____
_____
_____
_____

7) List five actions that could result in your getting dismissed from your job.

_____
_____
_____
_____
_____
_____
_____
_____

8) What is competence?

_____
_____
_____
_____
_____
_____
_____
_____

9) Define *reliable, accountable,* and *diligent.* Give one example of each.

_____
_____
_____
_____
_____
_____
_____

10) What does it mean to make a commitment to your job? Give one example of being committed and one example of not being committed.

_____

_____

_____

_____

_____

_____

11) What is a strong "work ethic" and why is it important to employers?

_____

_____

_____

_____

_____

_____

12) What should you do if you make a mistake?

_____

_____

_____

_____

_____

_____

13) Why are good attendance and punctuality so important?

_____

_____

_____

_____

_____

_____

14) What's a contingency plan? Give an example.

_____

_____

_____

_____

_____

_____
_____

15) Define _insubordination_ and give an example.

_____
_____
_____
_____
_____
_____
_____

16) What is corporate compliance, and why is it becoming even more important today than it has been in the past?

_____
_____
_____
_____
_____
_____
_____

17) List three examples of compliance issues.

_____
_____
_____
_____
_____
_____

18) What is a whistle blower?

_____
_____
_____
_____
_____
_____

19) What is confidentiality and why is it important?

_____
_____
_____

_____
_____
_____
_____

20) What is sexual harassment?

_____
_____
_____
_____
_____
_____

21) What is a hostile workplace?

_____
_____
_____
_____
_____
_____

22) What is a scope of practice and why is it important?

_____
_____
_____
_____
_____
_____

23) What is the difference between a license and a certification?

_____
_____
_____
_____
_____
_____

24) Define _conflict of interest_ and give an example.

_____
_____
_____

_____

_____

_____

_____

25) Discuss what is meant by "*You* are the company you work for."

_____

_____

_____

_____

_____

_____

26) What are corporate mission and corporate values? Why is it important for employees to support the mission and values of the company they work for?

_____

_____

_____

_____

_____

_____

_____

27) Define *discretion* and explain why it's important.

_____

_____

_____

_____

_____

_____

28) What is a vendor?

_____

_____

_____

_____

_____

_____

29) What are front-line workers and how do they influence a company's reputation?

_____

_____

_____

_____

_____

_____

_____

(Answers to Review Questions are at the end of the book.)

Chapter Two

Personal Traits of the Health Care Professional

CHAPTER OBJECTIVES

Having completed this chapter, students will be able to:

✔ Define *character* and *values,* and explain how these impact a person's reputation as a professional.

✔ List several examples of lack of character and of positive values in the workplace.

✔ Explain how character, values, and priorities define who we are as people and how we conduct our lives.

✔ List several questions to ask themselves when making difficult ethical decisions.

✔ Discuss the importance of their word being "good as gold."

✔ Give several examples of dishonest behaviors and describe the impact of dishonesty in the workplace.

✔ Explain how ethics and morals affect decision making and behavior.

CHARACTER AND WHO YOU ARE AS A PERSON

As mentioned in the Introduction, professionalism brings together who you are as a person and how you contribute those traits in the workplace. Before you can achieve success "doing" something, you have to "be" something, and being a health care professional depends greatly on who you are as person. It takes a long time to develop a good reputation, and only a split second to lose it. Much of this comes down to your core **character** and your **personal values.**

Webster's New World Dictionary of the American Language, College Edition, defines *character, values,* and *reputation.* Character is an "individual's pattern of behavior or personality," a "description of the traits or qualities of a person," the person's reputation, and his or her "moral constitution." Personal values are those things that have a "high degree of worth" to the individual, that are "highly desirable and worthy of esteem." A person's character and values give direction to one's behavior and ultimately result in one's **reputation**—"character in the view of the public or community, whether favorable or not."

Employers are becoming increasingly concerned about a lack of character and positive personal values in the workplace. Each year in businesses throughout the country, employees are responsible for stealing millions of dollars worth of goods from their employers and from other employees. Hidden video cameras in hospitals reveal employees stealing computers, office supplies, syringes, medications, and patients' personal possessions. Employees captured on videotape are some-times caught sleeping on the job, watching television, or engaging in sexual activity with a coworker. Would-be employees falsify information on job applications and overstate their education and work records. Countless numbers of fraudulent worker's compensation claims are filed each year. Arguments, fistfights, workplace violence, and sexual harassment are becoming more commonplace. Billing personnel routinely up-code claim forms to increase insurance reimbursement. Managers are increasingly involved in conflict-of-interest situations. Health care workers, dubbed "angels of mercy," murder dozens of hospitalized patients before they're discovered.

It's no wonder that employers are placing more and more emphasis on the character of their employees to help reduce theft, absenteeism, dishonesty, workplace violence, substance abuse, safety infractions, negligence, and low productivity. Increasingly, employers are hiring for character, praising for character, and promoting for character. Character reflects a person's **morals**—the capability of differentiating between right and wrong—and it influences **integrity** and **trustworthiness,** two key factors in professionalism.

How do character, values, reputation, morals, integrity, and trustworthiness apply to you as a person? How do they affect the way you approach your work? Do you know the difference between right and wrong? Are you honest? Can you be trusted?

REPUTATION

No single factor is more important in being recognized as a professional than a person's reputation. As mentioned above, it takes a long time to develop a good reputation and only a split second to lose it. After years of being an honest, law-abiding individual, all it takes is one dishonest act or a single incident of some other unprofessional behavior to shake people's confidence in you and lose their trust. This is why professionals must work hard each and every day to do what's right and to maintain the trust and respect of others.

If you've developed a pattern of behavior over the years based on lying, cheating, stealing, and taking advantage of other people, then changing your character at this point in your life is going to be quite a challenge. Our sense of acceptable behavior started at a very young age when our parents, and other influential people in our lives, began to teach us the difference between right and wrong. As children, we experimented with different kinds of behavior to see what reactions we would get. If those who raised us believed in discipline, we soon learned the consequences of "doing something bad." We were taught to get along with other children, to share our toys, to wash our hands before we ate, and to clean our rooms and make our beds. Unacceptable behavior resulted in "getting grounded" and losing privileges like playing outside with our friends or watching a favorite television program. Over the years, we learned to make **judgment** calls, to compare our options and decide which is best. We learned the concept of self-control and the importance of avoiding temptation. Through relationships with other people, we learned about fairness, respect, **ethics,** and loyalty. We learned to care, to give, and to appreciate. And before long, our character, values, and **priorities** begin to define *who* we are as people and *how* we conduct our lives.

JUDGMENT AND DECISION MAKING

As adults, we're faced with making multiple decisions every day—*what* to do, *why* to do it, *how* to do it, *when* to do it, *where* to do it, *whom* to do it with, and so on. Some of the decisions we must make are "small" ones—what to eat for breakfast, where to go for lunch, who to invite for dinner. But other decisions, especially those involving relationships with people, require much thought and carry significant consequences—how to resolve a disagreement, when to say "no," whom to ask for help.

Many questions must be considered when making decisions: What are my choices? How do the options compare with one another? What might happen? Who might be affected? How would it make me feel? How would my decision be viewed by other people? When the decisions you face involve your job, more questions arise: What would my supervisor think? How would my coworkers feel? Could I lose my job?

Most people have a **conscience**—a little voice that gnaws away at you, keeps you from sleeping at night, and constantly says, "You *know* this *isn't* the right thing to do!" Your conscience can be quite reliable in reminding you of the difference between right and wrong. When you're facing some really difficult ethical decisions, even more questions need to be considered. How would this look if it appeared in the newspapers? How would my children feel? Would my family support me? Could I look myself in the mirror? Would I be able to sleep at night?

The problem is, many people either have no conscience, have learned to ignore their conscience, or have become good at rationalizing their behavior. It starts with something small, like telling a lie or stealing some candy, and then grows and grows until it becomes a way of life. Eventually, dishonest and unethical behavior will be revealed but, in the meantime, countless people may be victimized.

The good news is that the majority of Americans are honest, law-abiding people with good character and sound moral values who sincerely want to do what's right in their lives. They face temptations but summon up the courage to say "No!" and they don't engage in dishonest behavior just because "everyone else is." Many people become angry with others but revert back to compassion and forgiveness.

They look out for themselves but still treat other people with fairness and respect. At times everyone needs some help exercising good judgment but, for the most part, most of us make the right decisions for the right reasons.

In the health care workplace, personal traits like character, values, morals, ethics, integrity, and trustworthiness are absolutely vital! If you were sick or injured, what kind of people would you want caring for you? If you owned a health care business, what kind of people would you want working for you? Let's take a closer look at character traits that are most essential for recognition as a health care professional.

RESPECT AND TRUST

A big part of professionalism is earning people's **respect,** which starts with their ability to trust you and the quality of the decisions you make. In today's society, we've become increasingly suspicious of other people. "Don't trust anyone!" is common advice. Unfortunately, that perspective gets reinforced each time we set ourselves up to believe in someone or depend on someone, only to end up disappointed or let down. The previous chapter discussed the importance of reliability and following through when someone is counting on you. When your word is "good as gold," your supervisor and coworkers know they can trust you to (1) be there when you're supposed to be, (2) perform the responsibilities of your job with competence, and (3) keep your promises and meet your obligations. Once trust is established and maintained over time, respect will likely follow. If you promised to give a coworker a ride to work, don't forget to pick him or her up. If you received training on a new procedure and your supervisor is trusting you to perform it properly, make sure you know what you're doing. If you tell a patient you'll relay a message to her nurse, follow through. If you want people to respect you, make sure you can be trusted.

HONESTY

Earning respect also relies greatly on being viewed as an honest person. As mentioned earlier, dishonesty has become highly visible in the health care workplace. The cost of health care is high enough without employers having to pay for extra supplies, food, and equipment stolen by its employees. Most health care workers would probably deny that they steal from their employers or patients. But theft goes well beyond stealing a computer or a patient's wallet. For example, if you manipulate your time card and get paid for more hours than you actually worked, that's theft. If you sleep on the job, take unauthorized breaks, or leave your work area without permission and still receive pay for that time, that's theft. If you make personal long-distance phone calls on a company phone, that's theft. If you use garage passes for yourself that were meant for visitors and guests, that's theft. If you take a sandwich off of a dietary catering cart waiting to be delivered to a luncheon meeting, that's theft. If you take supplies off of a patient's bedside table for yourself to use at home, that's theft. Anytime you take *anything* that doesn't belong to you without proper authorization, it can be construed as theft. Is a "free" sandwich or box of Q-tips worth losing your job over? What about an extra hour of pay that you didn't really deserve? This is where both honesty and good judgment enter the picture. Even if taking something that doesn't belong to you appears totally harmless, what might be the consequences?

The same is true with lying and cheating. Both are dishonest behaviors that can get you in big trouble. Little, seemingly harmless "white" lies usually snowball into big, complicated lies that can become difficult to manage. Lies are eventually uncovered and before long, people will wonder if they can believe *anything* you say. Being truthful is always the best approach and, sometimes, telling the truth takes courage. For example, what if you witness two coworkers leaving work early one afternoon after writing in a later time on their attendance sheets. If your supervisor notices their absence and asks if you know their whereabouts, what would you say? Would you be tempted to lie and say "No, I don't know where they are"? After all, you have to work with these two people every day, and if you "rat" on them, they might make life hard on you later. As just mentioned, telling the truth takes courage, and you're going to have to make decisions like this one on a regular basis. So let's examine the matter more closely. First of all, let's look at your coworkers. If you lie for them, will *they* respect *you?* Does it matter? After all, your coworkers are dishonest. They're stealing from the company—*your* company. Is their opinion of you so important that you're willing to lie for them? What about your supervisor? You could probably tell this lie and get away with it, but what if he or she found out? Is it worth losing your job over? Then there's you and your conscience. Who can you be sure will know you've told a lie? You, of course! If you tell this little "white" lie and get away with it, what's next? When you see someone stealing a syringe from the supply room, are you going to lie for that person, too? After all, syringes aren't all *that* expensive and there are plenty left anyway. Would you lie for someone stealing a computer? How about stealing personal possessions from a patient? Just where are you going to draw the line?

Listen to your conscience. You know what your coworkers did was wrong. And you know if you lie to your supervisor, that's wrong, too. So summon up the courage and tell the truth—and get a good night's sleep! If you do make a mistake and tell a lie, have the courage to admit it and accept the consequences. Corrective action or getting dismissed from your job would be a big price to pay for your dishonesty, but at least you'd learn a valuable lesson.

Cheating is another example of dishonest behavior that can result from giving in to temptation. Maybe you have a test to take and didn't have time to study. It would be so easy just to stick some notes in your pocket and refer to them during the test. After all, you can go back over the material later—after you've passed the test. If your instructor or supervisor finds out that you've cheated on the test, you'll be in big trouble. You could fail the course, lose your job, or both. And if you think your classmates will stand by quietly and let you get away with cheating, think again. They put the time in to study for the test and you didn't. As with stealing, cheating goes well beyond what you might typically think of. For example, if you use information from someone else's report and then call it your own work, that's cheating. If you're given too much change in the cafeteria line and you keep the extra money, that's cheating. If you call in sick when you really just want a day off, that's cheating. Can you cheat just a little and get away with it? Ask your conscience.

A very serious example of dishonest behavior is falsifying information, also known as **fraud.** As mentioned in the previous chapter, fraud is not only dishonest, it's illegal. Misrepresenting your education, credentials, or work experience on a job application, résumé, or other document is fraud. Billing an insurance company for a patient procedure that never occurred is fraud. Backdating a legal document, entering incorrect data on equipment maintenance records, and changing the results of a research study are all examples of fraud. As with stealing and cheating, there may be more to fraud than you realize. If you sign someone else's name without his or her permission, that's fraud. If you turn in a time card that's inaccurate, that's fraud. If you tell your supervisor you passed a competency assessment when you really didn't, that's fraud. Being convicted of fraud not only can cost you your job, it can cost you your freedom, too.

Ethics and Morals

Two other character traits that factor into recognition as a professional are your ethics and morals. Both play a major role in decision making and behavior. Do your ethics and morals support professionalism? For example, would you let someone outside your company borrow your ID badge so he or she could get an employee discount on purchases in the gift shop? Would you satisfy your curiosity by sneaking a peek at a confidential file that contains your supervisor's annual income or another student's grades? Would you skip work on a day when you knew your unit would be exceptionally busy? Would you threaten to report a coworker's mistake unless he or she covers for you on the next holiday? Would you date a coworker and then share the intimate details at work? Would you place an anonymous phone call to a local television station to get a coworker in trouble? Would you clock out for your best friend so she could leave early? Would you ask a coworker to clock out or lie for you?

If it seems like some of the examples of ethical and moral issues overlap with those involving lying, cheating, stealing, and other dishonest acts discussed earlier, your observations are correct. When it comes to dishonesty, it's hard to separate one type of unprofessional behavior from another. For example, failing to return the extra change to the cashier in the cafeteria line is not only cheating, it's theft. Sneaking a peek at your supervisor's salary or another student's grades is not only unethical, it's a breach of confidentiality. Clocking out for a friend is not only unethical, it's fraud.

The point is, every decision you make and every action you take can have a huge impact. One bad judgment call can erode someone's trust in you. One unethical decision can destroy your reputation. One illegal act can cause you to be fired from your job—or worse.

If you find yourself in a difficult situation weighing one option against another, and you're not quite sure which course of action to pursue, consider the following questions: Is it honest? Is it ethical? Does it reflect good character? Is it based on sound moral values? How would it affect my reputation? Would it damage the trust others have in me? Would I be respected for my decision? What would a professional do? What does my conscience tell me to do? What impact would my actions have on others?

This chapter could continue on with more examples of how character and values reflect who you are as a person and how your personal traits affect decision making and behavior in the workplace. But you already know what kind of person you are and you know the difference between right and wrong. You also know what's expected of health care professionals. Either you can choose to live up to those high standards, or you can try to slide by with less. No one can make that decision for you.

The next chapter explores working with others—how personality types, communication skills, and teamwork affect interpersonal relationships on the job.

GLOSSARY OF TERMS

character   a person's moral behavior and qualities

personal values   things of great worth and importance

reputation   a person's character, values, and behavior as viewed by others

morals   capability of differentiating between right and wrong

integrity   of sound moral principle

trustworthiness   ability to have confidence in the honesty, integrity, reliability of another person

judgment   comparison of options to decide which is best

ethics   standards of conduct and moral judgment

priorities   having precedence in time, order, and importance

conscience   moral judgment that prohibits or opposes the violation of a previously recognized ethical principle

respect   feeling or showing honor or esteem

fraud   intentional deceit through false information or misrepresentation

✐ EXERCISES

Complete the following.

1) If you owned a company, what kind of people would you want working for you? List five character traits that you would look for in your employees.

_____

_____

_____

_____

_____

_____

_____

_____

2) If you were a patient, what kind of people would you want caring for you? List five character traits of good caregivers.

_____

_____

_____

_____

_____

_____

_____

_____

3) Describe three times when you've demonstrated good character in your job.

_____

_____

_____
_____
_____
_____
_____
_____

4) If you asked three people who know you well, what would they say about your character?

_____
_____
_____
_____
_____
_____
_____
_____

5) List five ways to maintain a good reputation.

_____
_____
_____
_____
_____
_____
_____

6) Describe three strategies to convince coworkers you are trustworthy.

_____
_____
_____
_____
_____
_____
_____

7) List ten behaviors resulting from a lack of character. Indicate which behaviors could lead to dismissal from your job.

_____
_____
_____
_____

_____

_____

_____

_____

8) List two examples of employee theft that, at first glance, might not appear to be theft.

_____

_____

_____

_____

_____

_____

_____

_____

9) Describe a decision you had to make based on your personal ethics.

_____

_____

_____

_____

_____

_____

_____

_____

10) Describe a situation when someone lied to you. What happened and how did you feel?

_____

_____

_____

_____

_____

_____

_____

_____

11) Do people you work with respect you? Why or why not?

_____

_____

_____

_____

_____

_____

_____

✍ SELF-ASSESSMENT

Think about yourself and how you approach your work. Consider each of the following and check all that apply.

_____ 1) I demonstrate good character and personal values in my work.

_____ 2) I know the difference between right and wrong and apply my morals in decision making.

_____ 3) I work hard to maintain a good reputation.

_____ 4) People know they can trust me.

_____ 5) I avoid dishonest behaviors.

_____ 6) I would never steal from my employer.

_____ 7) I am truthful and do not tell lies.

_____ 8) I believe cheating is morally wrong.

_____ 9) My integrity is important to me.

_____ 10) I demonstrate good judgment by making sound decisions.

_____ 11) I listen to my conscience.

_____ 12) People respect me.

_____ 13) My word is good as gold.

_____ 14) I avoid giving in to temptations that could lead to unprofessional behavior.

_____ 15) I would never falsify information or misrepresent myself.

_____ 16) I maintain confidentiality.

_____ 17) I set high moral standards for myself and live up to them.

_____ 18) My job is a high priority in my life.

_____ 19) I always try to be fair in my dealings with other people.

✍ INDIVIDUAL NEXT-STEP ACTION PLANS

Based on your Self-Assessment, complete the following.

1) My strongest skills are:

_____

_____

_____

_____

_____

_____

_____

_____

2) My areas for improvement are:

_____

_____

_____

_____

_____

_____

_____

_____

3) Five things I plan to do to improve my skills:
   a) _____
   b) _____
   c) _____
   d) _____
   e) _____

✎ WHAT IF SCENARIOS

What would you do in the following situations?

1) You witness a coworker taking money from the petty cash box in your department. She says she needs to borrow the money to get her car fixed, and she'll pay it back when she gets her next paycheck. She reminds you that she did you a big favor when you first started your job and asks that you not report her to the supervisor.

_____

_____

_____

_____

_____

_____

_____

2) You need to have your time card signed by the end of the day. You know your supervisor would sign it, but she's tied up in a meeting and your shift ends in ten minutes.

_____

_____

_____
_____
_____
_____
_____

3) You have one more paper to turn in for a course you're taking that's required for your job. You kept the weekend open to write it, but an old friend calls and says he'll be in town for the weekend and would like to spend it with you. You know there won't be enough time both to write the paper and to visit with your friend. You just happen to have a copy of a paper that someone else wrote for the same course two years ago that earned a grade of "B." The course is being taught by a new instructor who would never know that you didn't write the paper yourself.

_____
_____
_____
_____
_____
_____
_____
_____

4) Your supervisor had asked you to attend a meeting in her place but you forgot to go. You know she'll be upset with you because she needs the information that was handed out. Someone else you know did go to the meeting and has agreed to give you copies of the handouts. When you hand the information to your supervisor, she asks, "So what did you think of the meeting?"

_____
_____
_____
_____
_____
_____
_____

5) A patient on your unit gets discharged. While cleaning the room for the next patient, you find an expensive watch in the drawer in the bedside table. It's a woman's watch and the former patient was a man.

_____
_____
_____
_____

_____

_____

_____

_____

6) When you open up your paycheck, you realize that you got paid for a day that you didn't work.

_____

_____

_____

_____

_____

_____

_____

7) You'd like to call your sister in Maine but can't afford the long-distance phone charge. The phone in your break room has long-distance access, and other workers have used it for personal calls without being questioned.

_____

_____

_____

_____

_____

_____

_____

_____

8) As a research assistant, your salary and the project you're involved in are funded by a federal grant. If the results of the research are positive, the grant and your job will get renewed for another year. The director of the research project asks you to help him change some of the data to indicate better results.

_____

_____

_____

_____

_____

_____

_____

_____

9) When it's time for your annual competency evaluation, your supervisor announces that you and your coworkers will be checking each other off. Your

coworkers get together and decide just to give each other a satisfactory evaluation without actually checking each person's competency level.

_____

_____

_____

_____

_____

_____

_____

_____

✍ REVIEW QUESTIONS

Answer each of the following.

1) Discuss what is meant by "Professionalism brings together who you are as a person and how you contribute those traits in the workplace."

_____

_____

_____

_____

_____

_____

_____

_____

2) Explain why employers are putting more emphasis on the character of their employees.

_____

_____

_____

_____

_____

_____

_____

_____

3) Define _character_ and list five character traits.

_____

_____

_____

_____
_____
_____
_____
_____

4) List five workplace problems that can be traced back to a lack of character among employees.

_____
_____
_____
_____
_____
_____
_____
_____

5) Define *reputation* and list five factors that influence it.

_____
_____
_____
_____
_____
_____
_____
_____

6) What is judgment?

_____
_____
_____
_____
_____
_____
_____
_____

7) What is a conscience and what role does it play in making decisions?

_____
_____
_____
_____
_____
_____

8) List three questions to ask yourself when making a difficult decision.

9) Explain why it's difficult to build trust but easy to lose it.

10) Explain what is meant by "A professional's word is good as gold."

11) Give two examples of cheating.

12) Explain why a "little white lie" doesn't remain "little" for long.

_____

_____

_____

_____

_____

_____

13) Define *fraud* and give two examples.

_____

_____

_____

_____

_____

_____

_____

_____

14) Give two examples of how morals and ethics can affect someone's reputation.

_____

_____

_____

_____

_____

_____

_____

_____

15) List three things you can do to earn people's respect.

_____

_____

_____

_____

_____

_____

_____

(Answers to Review Questions are at the end of the book.)

Chapter Three

Working with Others

CHAPTER OBJECTIVES

Having completed this chapter, students will be able to:

✔ Describe the concept of interdependence, and list several techniques to establish effective interpersonal relationships in the workplace.

✔ Explain why coworkers should be treated as customers.

✔ Discuss ways to demonstrate loyalty to their coworkers and to their employer.

✔ List ways to get to know their coworkers better and improve teamwork and interpersonal relationships.

✔ Discuss how personality differences can cause conflicts in the workplace.

✔ Define *diversity* and list examples of cultural differences.

✔ Explain the role of respect, good manners, and courtesy in the workplace.

✔ Describe why communication skills are the basis for effective relationships.

✔ Define *conflict resolution* and explain its importance.

✔ List the four styles of communication, identify which is most effective in conflict resolution, and describe the potential impact of each style.

✔ List the types of customers found in health care settings, and give several examples of good customer service.

Now that we've examined character traits and how they're applied in the workplace, it's time to discuss how health care professionals work with other people. How you interact with other people and the relationships you form with coworkers are the basis for success in the workplace. **Interdependence** is a key element in providing direct patient care and the many support services that comprise our health care system. No one person can do it all; only groups of people working together can get the job done and done well.

Professionals devote a lot of energy to establishing positive **interpersonal relationships,** and they treat one another in a caring, respectful manner. How you work with your colleagues helps mold your reputation as a professional. Valuing diversity, good manners and social skills, and effective customer service and interpersonal communication skills are all key factors in a professional work environment. Let's look at each of these to see how you get along with other people.

INTERPERSONAL RELATIONSHIPS WITH COWORKERS

If you're employed on a full-time basis, you probably spend as much time with your coworkers each day as you do with your family and friends. Nothing can make your job more pleasant or miserable than relationships at work. Think about the relationships you've had with people in the past. What made those relationships work or not work? People want to feel good about coming to work, and getting along well with others helps create a positive, enjoyable work environment.

Effective relationships are based on many of the factors discussed in the previous chapter—trust, honesty, ethics, and fairness. But working well with others requires several additional traits and interpersonal skills. For example, health care professionals are well versed in customer service techniques. Did you know that your coworkers are your customers, too? That might sound odd, but your coworkers are your "internal" customers. They deserve to be treated with the same respect and compassion that you would give your patients. Apply the same communication skills and conflict resolution techniques with your coworkers that you would use with other customers, and don't forget your manners!

An important part of effective interpersonal relationships at work is creating and maintaining a positive attitude and always looking for the best in situations. Professionals have an optimistic outlook. They see "the glass as half full, not half empty." They see opportunities and challenges, not just problems. They look for the best in people, give others the benefit of the doubt, and assume everyone is there to do his or her best. It's important to be viewed as a team player, to cooperate with others, and to contribute to the team effort. Smile every chance you get, say "hello" when you meet people in the hallways, and avoid creating a negative environment by whining, complaining, and questioning authority. Complainers "poison" the workplace and stir up discontent. If you get labeled as a complainer, you'll be viewed by management as a troublemaker and your opportunities for advancement will be limited.

Be **inclusive.** Rather than participating in **cliques,** invite people to join you and welcome their friendship. How do you feel when you're left out of a group? Excluding people can hurt their feelings. Keep in mind that you have a great deal of influence on how other people feel about themselves. A person's **self-esteem** and **self-worth** result from the feedback she gets from others. Help people recognize their strengths and abilities, support their growth and development, and celebrate their accomplishments with them.

Because health care workers are interdependent, it's important to share information openly. Unfortunately, some people hoard information because it gives them a sense of power over others. They have something you don't and it makes them feel important. An attitude like this is counterproductive to teamwork. Also share space, equipment, and supplies. Remember, you and your coworkers are all there for the same purpose—to serve your patients and other customers. There's no need for competition. Laugh at yourself, be a good sport, and maintain your sense of humor. Avoid arrogance and don't be a snob. Never "look down" on other people or treat someone in a demeaning way because he or she has less education, income, or "status" than you. There will always be people "above" you and "below" you in the hierarchy of your organization, and *every single person* is important in accomplishing the company's mission. Remember the golden rule and treat others as you want to be treated yourself. Gain satisfaction from your accomplishments but don't brag about them. Always acknowledge the achievements of others and credit their efforts.

Building effective relationships doesn't happen overnight. It's hard work and you have to hang in there. Be patient with yourself and with others, and be forgiving. No one is perfect—not even you! Get to know people better—you may see a whole different side of someone's personality and the many priorities he or she must balance. Let your coworkers get to know you better, too. When you form strong relationships, you can anticipate one another's needs and be there to help.

Part of professionalism and earning the respect of others is being **loyal** to those who have helped you. Health care professionals work in stressful environments. Part of interdependence means coworkers must be able to rely on one another for encouragement and emotional support. This is extremely important when the going gets rough. Sometimes it can be difficult to get the kind of emotional support you need from those who don't work in health care themselves. Even though family and friends want to help you, unless you've been there yourself, it's hard to relate to the stress of working with sick and injured people every day—and especially with critically ill children. Professionals are there for one another, to lend a helping hand or a shoulder to cry on. When someone you work with needs support, be ready to help. Most times it means just listening—and understanding.

While we're on the subject of loyalty, let's digress just a bit and talk about loyalty to your employer, too. In an earlier chapter, we discussed your responsibilities in representing the company that employs you. When you really think about it, you don't actually work for a company, you work for the *people* that manage the company. After all, companies are just legal entities that own assets such as buildings, property, and equipment. You don't work for a building, you work for people! Professionals can make that distinction, and they feel a sense of loyalty to the people they work *for* as well as those they work *with*. Even if you don't agree with all of management's policies or you feel as if you deserve more pay or better benefits, remember that management is providing you with employment and an opportunity to make a living. What can you do to demonstrate your appreciation for and loyalty to your employer? Of course, the most important thing is to always give your job your best effort and provide excellent customer service. Whenever you get the chance, express your appreciation to management and let managers know it makes you feel proud to be a part of the company. Managers and administrators are people, too, and they appreciate being appreciated. If your employer invests in your education and helps you acquire some new skills, pay the company back! How can you do that? By continuing to work for the company for a reasonable length of time after training rather than taking your new skills across town to go to work for the competition. A local competitor might offer you some extra pay to "jump ship," but remember who invested in your education to begin with and demonstrate your loyalty.

Someday you might need a letter of recommendation from your current employer. If management views you as a loyal employee, it can only help.

Now, back to our discussion about establishing strong interpersonal relationships with your coworkers. Offer to help someone else even if he or she has not asked you for help. When you've got a tough job to do or you're running late, isn't it a welcome relief to have someone walk up to you and say "Need a hand?" Be willing to rotate shifts and holidays—your coworkers will appreciate such consideration. Be willing to compromise on your own needs and make personal sacrifices for others. Sensitivity and kindness are rewarded many times over.

Learning to rely on one another is vital, especially in emergencies and other stressful situations. Gain an appreciation for the strengths, abilities, and personal traits that make each individual unique. Be familiar with contributions that others bring to the workplace so everyone can count on one another when the need arises. Volunteer to serve on committees to meet people from other areas and to establish relationships with them, too. Sign up for employer-sponsored classes and recreational activities. Join people during your lunch break and widen your circle of **colleagues.** You'll find there's **synergy** in working with other people. A group can accomplish so much more than people working independently as individuals. Relationships with colleagues can enrich your life and add a whole new dimension to friendship.

TEAMWORK

One of the most important aspects of interpersonal relationships is teamwork. Health care organizations are becoming increasingly dependent on teams and teamwork. In fact, many of the approaches to staffing newly restructured hospitals are based on "high performance work teams." Team members receive extra training in interpersonal and communication skills, negotiation and conflict resolution, delegation, and valuing diversity. Teams work with less supervision and take on additional responsibilities such as interviewing and selecting new team members, arranging work schedules, monitoring the use of resources, and evaluating each other's performance.

Employees who work in teams are often cross-trained to function as **multiskilled** workers. This means they're capable of performing more than one function, often in more than one discipline. For example, a housekeeper might be cross-trained to perform basic maintenance and repair duties. A nursing assistant might learn to draw blood and prepare specimens for laboratory analysis. A unit secretary might learn to admit patients and process bills. A maintenance worker might also acquire carpentry skills. Multiskilled workers who participate on teams tend to be highly productive. They can provide more services than individuals working independently and can enhance convenience for patients. They bring versatility and flexibility to the staffing plan, and they save the company some money in labor costs. Multiskilling has become a major trend among health care employers, and it's likely you will encounter this concept in your work, too. If you'd like to learn more about multiskilled health care workers, consider reading *Multiskilled Health Care Workers: Issues and Approaches to Cross-Training* (refer to the Supplemental Learning Resources section at the end of this book for ordering information).

Whether you work with the same team on an ongoing and daily basis, or with a variety of different teams to tackle short-term projects, team skills are vital for health care professionals. Think about some of the teams you've participated on. Which teams worked well together and which ones did not, and why? Serving on a team can present all kinds of challenges, and it requires some special skills. Having to achieve, **consensus** when agreement is called for can be a big challenge. Consensus is more than just "voting" on different options and "majority rules." With majority rules, there are winners and there are losers—the majority wins and the minority loses. The objective of consensus, however, is to arrive at a win-win resolution. Through group interaction, team members strive to select an option that *all* members agree to support. As you might imagine, that can be quite a challenge. But setting up win-win situations and operating by consensus are the underpinning of good teamwork. Good communication skills are absolutely mandatory—a topic discussed later in this chapter.

Developing effective teamwork takes time, especially among diverse groups of people with different personalities, values, and communication styles. But being part of a smooth-running team can be one of the most exhilarating experiences for health care professionals. Work with your teammates to establish **group norms**—guidelines that can help the group function well. This includes such things as the following: (1) Every member is expected to participate in decision making, (2) each person's opinion will be listened to and respected, (3) all members will do their share of the work, and (4) no one may leave until the team's work has been completed.

Teamwork also involves good leadership skills, as well as good "followership" skills, because both roles are very important.

PERSONALITY PREFERENCES

Just as you are a unique individual with your own personality and preferences, so are all of the other people with whom you come in contact. Personality types vary widely, and they influence how people interact with one another and how they participate (or don't participate) in a group setting. Personality types also affect how people size up situations, make decisions, and approach their work.

Learn as much as you can about your own personality type, and gain some insight into the personality types of the people with whom you work. The more you

know about someone's personality, the better you will understand that person and
be able to work with, and communicate with, him or her. The Myers-Briggs Type
Indicator (MBTI) is a well-known process for identifying different personality
types. There are many other personality inventories available, but the MBTI has
been in use for many years, and provides an accurate, reliable method for identifying and comparing differences in personality preferences. A valuable feature of the
MBTI is the research that's been conducted to demonstrate how different personality types can best work together in the workplace.

How much do you know about your own personality type and those of the people you work with? Some people are "what if?" types. They like to brainstorm, use
their imaginations, and come up with new ideas. What if? people have difficulty
actually implementing a new idea because, once the idea has been conceived, they
would prefer to move on to thinking up the next new idea rather than continuing to
work on the first one. On the other hand, people with the opposite personality type
don't enjoy the what if? phase. They prefer having someone else come up with the
idea and then turn it over to them to coordinate the implementation phase. Obviously, you need both types of people to come up with good ideas and get them im-
plemented. Another way of looking at personality differences is the introvert/
extrovert. These are only two examples of differences in personalities. Learn all you
can to help you identify differences and be able to use those differences to everyone's advantage in the workplace.

Diversity

Differences among people go well beyond personality types. Other examples of **diversity** include differences in gender, age, race, culture, ethnic background,
lifestyle preferences, socioeconomic status, and physical condition. The United
States is a multicultural nation, composed of people from different cultures with a
variety of personal values, communication styles, and work ethics. Professionals
learn how to work with all kinds of people and to make the most of differences.
Learning to work with people who are different from you presents some challenges
but can also be quite rewarding. Just like with what if? kinds of people and their
opposites, diversity allows us to play upon our differences and to use everyone's
strengths to the best advantage.

The workplace requires a variety of people to get the work done. For example, if you're helping to write a new policy for your department, you might look at
the situation differently than someone who is much younger or older than yourself.
A young, single woman might have a different perspective than an older, married
man. Someone from an Hispanic culture might place a greater value on a particu-

lar issue in the policy than someone from an Asian culture. All points of view must be taken into consideration to accommodate our diverse population.

In health care, another type of culture is the occupation in which you work. Registered nurses, for example, have a culture based on their educational background, where they work, who they work with, what functions they perform, and the knowledge and abilities they possess. Physicians have a culture too, as well as pharmacists, medical technologists, secretaries, maintenance workers, and environmental services personnel. In many health care organizations, there's a visible hierarchy based on these cultures and sometimes it causes problems. As mentioned above, cross-training has become a major trend in health care. Because multiskilled workers are trained to provide more than one function, they often work in more than one area. They may encounter multiple cultures and may not feel totally accepted or comfortable in any of them. This is also true of some of the new types of jobs that are emerging in restructured hospitals. For example, patient care assistants (PCAs) or patient care technicians (PCTs) are a relatively new type of worker referred to as "nurse extenders." They aren't actually nurses but they work in assistant roles. Because PCAs and PCTs have less education than registered nurses (RNs), function at a lower skill level, and lack RN credentials, they don't fit into the RN culture. Often referred to as "unlicensed assistive personnel," PCAs and PCTs may experience some difficulty fitting in and feeling like part of the team. The same may be true for housekeepers, transportation aides, phlebotomists, and other types of non-RN workers assigned to patient care units. This also occurs in other areas, too—anytime someone "different" enters the group.

Experiencing a hard time fitting in and being accepted by other cultures is a common problem in dealing with diversity. But do differences *have* to pose such difficult challenges? Think about it. Does it really matter if your coworkers are younger or older than you, of a different gender, or from a different race or ethnic group? All of you might have to work a little harder at getting to know one another and figuring out the best way to accommodate your differences and make the most of them. But the point is, you're all there for the same purpose—to provide high-quality health care and support services. Focusing on the mission of patient care gives diverse groups of workers some "common ground" to build upon. If you find yourself in a situation where you've been placed in a culture that feels uncomfortable to you, hang in there.

Learn as much about the other cultures as possible and let others learn about yours. Let people know what you're capable of doing. Establish trust, build strong relationships, and work hard to develop a team spirit. Remember the earlier discussion about inclusion. When someone from a different culture gets placed within *your* culture, do your best to make them feel welcome. After all, nurses need housekeepers, PCAs need nurses, maintenance workers need secretaries, housekeepers need maintenance workers. Everyone needs everyone else. And your patients need all of you.

RESPECT

In the previous chapter, we discussed the role that character and behavior play in earning the respect of others. Now we're going to examine the factors involved in *you* respecting *others*.

Regardless of whether you're working with people just like yourself or different from yourself, respect is the basis for getting along well with others. Once you understand how people differ from one another, and you realize that there are no "good" people or "bad" people—just different people, you can learn to respect everyone regardless of his or her differences.

Think about yourself. If your personality, culture, or opinions are different from those of another person, don't you still want that person to respect you? People have a right to be different because we live in a democracy. You have a right to your opinions and other people have a right to theirs, assuming that laws are not violated and no one gets hurt or victimized in the process. Your job as a professional is to respect differences and the people who possess them. Show respect for everyone, regardless of their job title, background, cultural heritage, and so forth. Go out of your way to be especially kind to people who work in service and support roles. The "health care culture" seems to place more value on its highly educated, professionally credentialed clinical caregivers such as RNs and doctors. Service and support workers often feel they're at the bottom of the ladder. All too often, they're treated as if they're almost invisible. As a result, they sometimes feel underappreciated and taken for granted. (If you're one of these workers yourself, you already understand this point.) Acknowledge their efforts and let them know how much you value the work they do. Until you've walked in someone else's shoes, you have no idea all that his or her job involves.

Draw upon your character traits to show your respect for others. Be sincere and sensitive to other people's needs. Be considerate, kind, and sympathetic. Never ridicule someone, or embarrass or make them "feel dumb." Don't participate in gossip, pry into people's personal affairs, or be judgmental about how someone chooses to live his or her life. Respect the choices that other people make, even when you don't understand those choices yourself. If someone tells you something in confidence, maintain that confidentiality.

Respect a person's determination to do something on his or her own without your assistance. When people come to you for advice, be honest and remember how much influence you might have on the decisions they make. Respect people's privacy, personal possessions, and space. Respect people's health—don't come to work sick and spread your germs to others. Respect people's time and don't keep them waiting unnecessarily.

Keep your personal matters personal, and avoid dealing with personal problems while you're at work. If you must make a personal telephone call, keep your voice low so you don't distract other people around you. Better yet, wait for a break and use a telephone outside your work area. Don't chatter away mindlessly about non-work-related topics and interrupt other people from getting their work done. Don't bring things to work to sell and don't spend work time buying things from other employees. Always respect the fact that people come to work to get things done. It's good to practice your social skills with coworkers—but only during breaks and after hours.

If you're having a problem with a particular person and an attitude, behavior, or action he or she has taken, show respect by discussing the situation directly with the person first. Avoid taking matters to a supervisor until you've tried to resolve the problem yourself. If someone were having a problem with something you did, wouldn't you appreciate him or her coming directly to you first rather than to your boss?

Always respect authority. Even if you dislike your supervisor as a person, or you find fault with his or her job performance, it's still important to show respect for his or her experience and position within the organization.

MANNERS

Often, demonstrating respect comes down to having good **manners.** As young children, most of us learned manners from our parents and from other influential people in our lives. But all too often in today's society, manners and common courtesy fall by the wayside.

Manners are standards of behavior based on thoughtfulness and consideration of others. Be aware of, and sensitive to, other people's needs. Courtesy and small considerations can make a big difference. For example, ask others before adjusting the temperature of the room or playing music on the radio. Return borrowed items as soon as possible and in the same condition as when you borrowed them. If you break something you've borrowed, offer to repair or replace it at your own expense. Don't expect other people to clean up after you. Keep your own work area neat and orderly so it doesn't become an eyesore for others. Avoid putting up risqué calendars or other personal items that might offend someone else.

Say "please," and always acknowledge your appreciation when someone does something nice for you by saying "thank you." When someone has done something really special for you, send him or her a thank-you note or small gift. When someone you know joins a group you're with, introduce that person to the others. Be kind to strangers and try to make them feel welcome. Listen while other people are talking; don't interrupt them.

Hold doors open for people. When you see someone struggling to carry something heavy, run up and help them. If you notice someone who looks lost, ask if you can help him or her find the way. If several people are waiting for an elevator, let others go first and wait for the next one. If you're in a crowded room with limited seating, offer your seat to someone else. If your supervisor or a coworker invites you to lunch as his or her guest, don't order the most expensive item on the menu! When going through a banquet line, make sure you leave enough food for those in line behind you. If you're invited to a meeting or another event that involves a meal, be sure to notify the person organizing the event as to whether or not you'll be attending.

Good manners and common courtesy are just "common sense" for health care professionals. Watch for opportunities to display good manners with everyone you encounter.

COMMUNICATION SKILLS AND CONFLICT RESOLUTION

Just because you have good interpersonal skills, treat people with respect, and use good manners doesn't guarantee you'll get along with every person in every situation. In fact, you can pretty much count on some interpersonal conflicts with the people you work with. First of all, everyone's working in a stressful environment. When you're under pressure or feeling rushed, you don't always do your best in communicating well with others. And second, because of the diverse types of people you encounter, you cannot help but experience some difficulties getting along with everyone. You don't have to be best buddies with each and every coworker. In fact, there may be a few people you'd rather not work with at all. But because you can't choose your coworkers, and you can't change them either, you must find a way to get along with one another. Good communication skills can really help.

How effective are your communication skills? Are you good at **conflict resolution?**

Communication is the basis for teamwork and interpersonal relationships. You must be able to communicate effectively to get along with people and to complete your work appropriately. Communication is a two-way process. Messages are sent and received. Both aspects of the process must work well to support good communication.

Often when communication breaks down, it's because the person receiving the message isn't listening well to the person sending the message. Good listening skills are vital. It's important not only to *listen* to someone but also actually to *hear* what that person has to say. Most of us need to improve our listening skills. Learn to listen carefully and concentrate on the message so that you fully understand the other person's point of view. Repeat what he or she has said in your own words to make sure you received the message accurately. It's tempting to only "half-listen" while you're thinking about how you are going to respond. But if you do that, it's likely you'll miss part of the message. Always ask the other person for clarification when you don't fully understand what he or she is saying. Or ask the person to state the message again in different words. Observe the person's body language—the nonverbal messages and the tone of voice—to gather even more information.

Also hone your skills at sending messages to other people. Be clear and concise, and use terms your listener can easily understand. Give examples as further explanation. Don't get frustrated if the other person just "doesn't seem to get it." Hang in there and keep trying. If the conversation seems to be going nowhere, ask a third person to help out.

There are four basic styles of communication: aggressive, passive, passive-aggressive, and assertive. Let's use an example to examine each style and see which one works best in resolving conflicts. You and a coworker both want Christmas Day off. Both of you have relatives arriving in town and wish to spend time with them. After discussing the holiday schedule, it becomes obvious that one of you must work.

Using an *aggressive* style of communication, you say, "I've worked here longer than you so I deserve this day off! Besides, you don't have any children and I do!" Your coworker replies, "You got Thanksgiving Day off and I had to work. So I deserve Christmas Day off more than you! And besides, your children are adults now and my grandchildren are coming in for Christmas!" You reply, "Why do you always have to insist on getting your own way? Every time we do a schedule, you complain!" "I complain?" your coworker responds. "You're the one who always refuses to work overtime!" You can imagine where the "conversation" goes from here. With aggressive communication, the conflict usually gets worse. The sender (you, in this example) expresses his opinion honestly but does so in a way that fails to show any respect or consideration for the receiver. The receiver (your coworker, in this example) becomes defensive and fights back. Before long, anger has taken over, other issues enter the conversation, and the conflict escalates into aggressive behavior. The situation can turn violent, and shouting or fistfights might occur. Did anyone "win" in this situation? Let's try a different approach.

Using a *passive* style of communication, you say, "Well, I guess if you want Christmas Day off, I'll just have to work. Maybe my kids can come back for Easter and I can spend some time with them then." With passive communication, the sender (you) fails to express his opinion honestly and demonstrates no self-respect. He just turns into a floor mat to be walked upon! The receiver "won." He got his needs met. But the sender "lost." In fact, he comes off looking pretty pitiful. Let's try again.

Using *passive-aggressive* communication, you say, "Well, I guess if you want Christmas Day off, I'll just have to work. Maybe my kids can come back for Easter and I can spend some time with them then." Then, as soon as you get the chance, you do something sneaky to "get even." Maybe you send your supervisor an anonymous note saying your coworker takes longer breaks than he's allowed to. Or you spread malicious gossip about the coworker behind his back. After all, there are lots of ways to get even. Maybe it will make you feel better. With passive-aggressive communication, the sender (you) still fails to express his opinion honestly and demonstrates no self-respect. But then, to make matters worse, he does something underhanded and dishonest. Once again, the approach didn't work. Let's try one more time.

Using *assertive* communication, you say, "Well, we both want the day off. I'm sure you'd like to spend Christmas Day with your grandchildren. After all, you had to work Thanksgiving, didn't you? On the other hand, because I've worked here twice as long as you, I do have seniority. And my children are really looking forward to spending the day together as a family. So how can we work this out?" With assertive communication, the sender (you) states his opinion honestly but in a way that shows respect and consideration for the other person. It presents the best opportunity for both people to work together, to compromise, and to come up with a solution that's acceptable to both of them. It's a win-win situation—which is the goal of conflict resolution.

After reading this book up to this point, it should be obvious that assertive communication is the *only* acceptable communication style for health care professionals. You must have enough self-respect to state your needs honestly and not allow yourself to be walked on and pitied. But you must also respect your coworker's needs.

Assertive communication takes practice. Maybe you're not used to standing up for yourself when someone disagrees with you. Or maybe aggressive communication has been your style in the past. Hopefully, you're not a passive-aggressive person! Work on developing your assertive communication skills. Observe how other people deal with conflicts and the results they get. Then keep practicing your own skills.

Learn to "choose your battles wisely." Decide which conflicts are really worth tackling and which you ones you should just "let go." Some battles aren't worth the effort. And be careful! Just because you're taking an assertive approach, there's no guarantee the other person will, too. Someone may turn aggressive on you. When confronting a "difficult" person, make sure you can get out of the room quickly if you need to. If there's any concern about your physical safety, make sure there is someone else nearby who can come to your aid if necessary. Remember it's a crazy world out there. You never know when someone might be carrying a weapon or be passive-aggressive.

When you decide to confront someone, make sure you have all the facts first—complete and accurate information. Give the other person the benefit of the doubt until you've fully investigated the matter. Don't proceed on assumptions that may not be true. Don't go off "half-cocked" only to regret later something you've said or done. Stay calm, keep your anger and tone of voice in check, and arrange a suitable time and place to discuss differences. Listen carefully and make sure the other person understands your point of view, too. Aim for a win-win situation whenever possible. Once you fully understand the other person's point of view and he or she understands yours, there may be a middle ground where both of you can compromise and feel like your needs have been met.

When you have a conflict with a coworker, resolve it. Procrastination only makes things worse. Remember that you cannot change other people; only they can change themselves. Your job is to make your best effort at communicating appropriately. If necessary, ask someone else with good conflict resolution skills to serve as an intermediary.

If your supervisor is the "difficult person," proceed cautiously! Remember to respect his or her position of authority. Weigh the pros and cons of addressing the situation head-on or just learning to live with it. If you decide to discuss the matter with your supervisor, plan in advance what you're going to say, how you're going to say it, and what response you'll give to how he or she might react. Practice delivering the message in advance, and consider role-playing the situation first with someone you trust. Listen carefully, watch for a win-win resolution, and be open to receiving some constructive feedback that might help you form a more positive relationship with your supervisor in the future. If the matter is still unresolved and you cannot adjust to accepting it and moving forward, consider talking with a human resource representative or another person in authority in your department. If the situation is serious and cannot be resolved, you may need to transfer into another position.

Effective communication and conflict resolution skills will serve you well in all aspects of your life and, with practice, you'll just keep getting better and better.

Before moving on to the last part of this chapter, a few more comments need to be made about communication skills. So far, we've focused on verbal communication because of its importance in interpersonal relationships. But no discussion of communication skills would be complete without also addressing written communication and public speaking skills, as well as grammar.

The ability to communicate well in writing is certainly important, and most everyone can benefit from sharpening his or her writing skills. Even if your job doesn't involve extensive writing, how you express yourself through written communication still has an impact on being recognized as a professional. If you have difficulty with writing, spelling, or punctuation, get some help. Take a course, do some self-study, or work one-on-one with a basic skills instructor. Make sure you can write out telephone messages, notes to coworkers and your supervisor, and construct basic memos and letters should the need arise. If your job involves recording data on charts or other kinds of forms, make sure your writing is legible and your entries are accurate. If writing reports or preparing handouts for meetings is part of your responsibility, you'll need some higher-level writing skills to help you organize information and present it in an appropriate format.

Spelling is important, especially in health care. With medical terms, changing just one letter in a word can change the entire meaning. If you fill out forms to order tests or treatments for patients, order patient supplies, or process bills or other kinds of paperwork, make sure you can spell terms correctly.

Few challenges in life are more anxiety producing than having to get up in front of a group of people and make a presentation. But public speaking skills are important, especially if your job requires you to give updates at meetings, make announcements to the rest of the staff, or teach coworkers something new. Becoming comfortable with public speaking is like facing any other fear—the more you do it, the better you'll get, and the more comfortable it will become. Start out small, with a group of supportive people, and build from there. And remember, most of the people in the audience will be glad it's you up there talking instead of them!

Grammar is also an important aspect of good communication skills. This topic will be addressed in the next chapter dealing with your *image* as a health care professional.

CUSTOMER SERVICE

The final topic in this chapter discusses getting along not only with your coworkers, but also with all customers in your workplace. Depending on your job, you may deal with workers from other departments and with patients, visitors, guests, and vendors. You may also interact with doctors, some of whom are employees of your organization and others who are not. All of these different types of people are considered customers. The factors that define effective interpersonal relationships with coworkers also affect customer service and how you relate to the people you come in contact with each day. Like coworkers, your customers are a highly diverse group of people. They represent all personality types and a wide variety of differences. Some will be easy to get along with and others will be difficult. Some will appreciate your efforts whereas others will not. But, *all* customers deserve to be treated with respect and good manners.

Effective communication skills and conflict resolution techniques are extremely important in customer service. Equally important is knowing what it takes to "satisfy" customers and maintain that satisfaction. Let's start with a closer look at patients as customers.

As mentioned earlier, when people become patients, they're vulnerable and at their worst. They don't feel well, and they may be anxious, worried, confused, and overwhelmed with the medical experience. Many patients feel helpless, having to turn themselves over to people who will make decisions about their care. They're concerned about what might happen to them, how their lives will be affected, how their children and spouse will get along without them if they become hospitalized, and a whole host of other issues. Patients need reassurance and confidence that they are in good hands. How you look, communicate, and behave can have a tremendous impact on their feeling of security. Some of these factors will be addressed in the next chapter.

Remember what you've learned about valuing differences and diversity. These concepts apply to patients and other customers, too. It's not your place to be judgmental. Regardless of whether a patient is wealthy, poor, homeless, elderly, gay, or a criminal, each one deserves to be treated with respect. Respect their privacy and the confidentiality of their personal and medical information. Protect their dignity, self-respect, and personal possessions. Refer to patients as "Mr." or "Ms." Be compassionate, caring, and empathetic. Anticipate your patients' needs and be prepared to meet them. No request or concern is too trivial. However, if a patient asks you for a drink, food, medication, or assistance walking to the restroom, *never* fulfill the request yourself unless your job already involves these duties! Always refer any matter that is outside of your scope of practice to the patient's nurse or another caregiver on the unit, and then make sure the appropriate person follows through.

When communicating with patients, use terms they can understand. If they ask you a question you are not capable of answering or not authorized to answer, refer the question to the appropriate person. Never pick up a patient's chart and read it unless that's part of your job, and don't divulge information about a patient's medical status to the patient's family members, clergy, or other visitors.

As mentioned above, doctors are customers, too. As with other customers, you'll encounter doctors with different kinds of personality types and communication styles. Some will take an interest in you, show you things, and explain procedures as they do them. Others will treat you as if you're invisible. One day a doctor will be friendly, and the next day he or she will remain aloof. Sometimes doctors can be intimidating. Always keep in mind that doctors are people, too. Much of the time they're under a great deal of stress and they're almost always in a hurry. If a doctor appears angry, it may or may not have anything to do with you. Occasionally a doctor may ask you to do something that's outside of your scope of practice. He or she may mistake you for a different type of worker or may not be familiar with your training and job duties. If this happens, speak up! Don't just go ahead and do something you aren't qualified to do because a doctor asked you to. Say, "That's not within my scope of practice. I'll go get someone who can help you." If you keep on your toes and apply your best customer service skills, you'll likely get along just fine with doctors.

Visitors and guests in your facility are also customers. They, too, are a diverse group of people. Some may be lost and stressed out, trying to find a loved one and worried about his or her condition. Others may be in the building to attend a meeting, participate in a training session, or keep an appointment with a manager or administrator. Probably the most frequent request you'll get from visitors and guests is help with directions. If you work in a large building, make sure you know your way around so you can give good directions to other people. If you have the time or are headed in that direction anyway, offer to walk with someone to make sure he or she gets to the destination. If someone is waiting to see your supervisor or someone else in your area and you have access to coffee or a soft drink, offer the person some. If someone's pager goes off, direct him or her to the nearest telephone. If you know someone is going to have to wait for a while, let the person know and explain why. Do whatever you can to make visitors and guests comfortable. It's amazing how much your customers will appreciate even a small gesture of kindness.

The last group of customers is vendors. As mentioned previously, vendors are people who work for companies that your company does business with. Vendors might be salespeople from a patient supply or equipment company. They might be insurance agents or drug company representatives. They might work for advertising agencies or temporary services. Just like other customers, they too should be treated with respect and good manners.

There are many factors involved in interpersonal relationships with employees and in providing good customer service. The next chapter explores even more aspects of professionalism.

GLOSSARY OF TERMS

interdependence   the need to rely on one another

interpersonal relationships   connections between or among people

inclusive   tending to include everyone

cliques   small, exclusive circles of people

self-esteem   belief in oneself, self-respect

self-worth   importance and value in oneself

loyal   faithful to people that one is under obligation to defend or support

colleagues   fellow workers in the same profession

synergy   energy created through cooperative action

multiskilled   cross-trained to perform more than one function, often in more than one discipline

> **consensus**   decision that all members agree to support
>
> **group norms**   standards, models, or patterns for a group
>
> **diversity**   differences, dissimilarities, variations
>
> **manners**   standards of behavior based on thoughtfulness and consideration of other people
>
> **conflict resolution**   overcoming disagreements between two or more people

EXERCISES

Complete the following.

1) Think about a group of people you interact with on an ongoing basis at work, at school, or in your personal life. How strong are the relationships among individuals in the group? List the factors that support and do not support strong relationships within your group.

_____

_____

_____

_____

_____

_____

_____

2) Describe a group you've worked with where the group as a whole was able to accomplish much more than the individuals working alone.

_____

_____

_____

_____

_____

_____

_____

3) Describe your vision of an ideal, enjoyable workplace.

_____

_____

_____

_____

_____

_____

_____

_____

4) Have you ever been part of a clique? Have you ever been left out of a clique? How did it make you feel to be included or excluded?

_____

_____

_____

_____

_____

_____

_____

5) Think back to a situation where you've given someone "the benefit of the doubt." What happened and why? Describe a situation where someone has given you the benefit of the doubt. What happened and why?

_____

_____

_____

_____

_____

_____

_____

_____

6) Describe a situation when you've helped strengthen someone's self-esteem and self-worth.

_____

_____

_____

_____

_____

_____

_____

7) Describe a situation where you've felt uncomfortable trying to fit in to a different culture.

_____

_____

_____

_____
_____
_____
_____
_____

8) Describe three examples of bad manners that you've observed. How could the behaviors have been better?

_____
_____
_____
_____
_____
_____
_____
_____

9) Think back to a team you've participated on. Did the team have group norms? If yes, what were they? Were these norms the result of a conscious effort or did they just emerge? Did having norms help? If the team did not have group norms, did the lack of norms hinder the group from accomplishing its goals? Why or why not?

_____
_____
_____
_____
_____
_____
_____
_____

10) Describe your own personality type. Identify another person whose personality is different from yours and list three ways that differences might cause conflicts between the two of you. List three ways these differences might complement one another.

_____
_____
_____
_____
_____
_____
_____

11) Think back to the last time you had a conflict with someone and tried to resolve it. Describe the situation and the communication style you used. Was it effective? Why or why not?

_____

_____

_____

_____

_____

_____

_____

_____

12) Identify two situations when you had to "choose your battles wisely." What happened?

_____

_____

_____

_____

_____

_____

_____

_____

13) Describe a time when you've been involved in a win-win resolution. What happened and why?

_____

_____

_____

_____

_____

_____

_____

_____

14) Think back to the last time you were a customer of the health care system. How did you feel about being a patient? What customer service skills did you observe? What customer service skills were missing? How could the experience have been more positive?

_____

_____

_____

_____

_____

_____

_____

✎ SELF-ASSESSMENT

Think about yourself and how you approach your work. Consider each of the following and check all that apply.

_____ **1)** I work hard at establishing positive interpersonal relationships.

_____ **2)** I treat my coworkers as internal customers.

_____ **3)** I'm optimistic and try to see the glass as half full rather than half empty.

_____ **4)** I have a positive attitude; I avoid whining and complaining.

_____ **5)** I go out of my way to include people rather than exclude them.

_____ **6)** I help strengthen the self-esteem and self-worth of my coworkers.

_____ **7)** I share information with my colleagues.

_____ **8)** I have a good sense of humor and can laugh at myself.

_____ **9)** I'm loyal to coworkers and to the company that employs me.

_____ **10)** I'm considerate and sensitive to the needs of my coworkers; I'm there for them when they need me.

_____ **11)** I contribute my best to team efforts.

_____ **12)** I'm willing to compromise to help reach consensus.

_____ **13)** I'm aware of my own personality type; I know how it's similar to and different from the personality types of my coworkers.

_____ **14)** I respect and value diversity and differences among people.

_____ **15)** I help other people fit into my culture.

_____ **16)** My behaviors reflect the respect I have for my coworkers and other customers.

_____ **17)** I keep my personal matters private and I respect the privacy of others.

_____ **18)** I would never ridicule people, embarrass them, or make them feel dumb.

_____ **19)** I appreciate and acknowledge the efforts of service and support workers.

_____ **20)** If I have a problem with someone, I try to resolve the problem with the person first before taking the matter to a supervisor.

_____ **21)** I always use good manners.

_____ **22)** I listen well and have effective communication skills.

_____ **23)** When dealing with conflicts, my assertive style of communicate helps me arrive at win-win resolutions.

_____ **24)** I choose my battles wisely; if one's not worth fighting, I let it go.

_____ **25)** I treat all customers with respect and consideration.

_____ **26)** I do everything I can to support good customer service.

✐ INDIVIDUAL NEXT-STEP ACTION PLANS

Based on your Self-Assessment, complete the following.

1) My strongest skills are:

_____

_____

_____

_____

_____

_____

_____

_____

2) My areas for improvement are:

_____

_____

_____

_____

_____

_____

_____

_____

3) Five things I plan to do to improve my skills:

a) _____

b) _____

c) _____

d) _____

e) _____

✐ WHAT IF SCENARIOS

What would you do in the following situations?

1) Your supervisor has given you a project to complete. There's no way you can possibly get it done, and done well, by yourself in time to meet the deadline.

Your coworkers have expressed willingness to help, but you're used to working alone.

_____
_____
_____
_____
_____
_____
_____
_____

2) Three coworkers approach you, angry about a new policy. They're rounding up support to complain to the administration and want you to get involved.

_____
_____
_____
_____
_____
_____
_____
_____

3) A new person joins your work group. She's much older than everyone else and no one seems to like her. It's time to go to lunch and your coworkers leave her behind.

_____
_____
_____
_____
_____
_____
_____
_____

4) At an employee recognition dinner, the head of your company calls you to the stage to praise you for creating a new inventory tracking system. Although three of your coworkers helped you a lot, their names aren't mentioned.

_____
_____
_____
_____

_____

_____

_____

5) Your company offers a six-month, part-time equipment repair course free of charge to employees. Those who enroll attend the classes on paid time. The company also pays the fee for course graduates to become certified as equipment repair technicians. After completing the course and becoming certified, you spot a newspaper advertisement recruiting certified equipment repair technicians for a company that competes with your employer. According to the ad, the pay at the other company is slightly higher than the pay at your company.

_____

_____

_____

_____

_____

_____

_____

_____

6) You've been on call the last two weekends and it's your turn to be off. At the last minute, a coworker asks if there's any way you could take call for her this weekend. Her brother was seriously injured in a car accident and needs her to help take care of his children for a couple of days. You don't have any plans yourself, but you've already taken call two weekends in a row.

_____

_____

_____

_____

_____

_____

_____

7) A team has been formed to design a new care plan for lung transplant patients. The team's goal is to streamline the process of moving patients from surgery, to a patient care unit, to discharge, and then follow up after they've returned home. Team members include registered nurses, patient care assistants, respiratory therapists, surgical technologists, and home care personnel. Team meetings seem to be going nowhere. Several personalities clash, people disagree on how to get started, and no one listens to each other.

_____

_____

_____
_____
_____
_____
_____
_____

8) One of your coworkers is really beginning to annoy you. He takes longer breaks than he's supposed to and seems to disappear when there's work to be done. This morning, he has kept a patient waiting for twenty minutes while he made several personal phone calls. When you remind him he has a patient waiting, he says, "Mind your own business! I'll get to him when I'm ready!"

_____
_____
_____
_____
_____
_____
_____
_____

9) You hear through the grapevine that a coworker has been spreading gossip about you. You're so angry that, as soon as she walks in the room, you're anxious to tell her just what you think of her behavior.

_____
_____
_____
_____
_____
_____
_____
_____

10) One of your coworkers is on corrective action for misspelling several medical terms on patient records. Unless she passes a medical terminology test by the end of the month, her job could be in jeopardy. She's lost her confidence and isn't sure if she can do it.

_____
_____
_____
_____
_____

_____
_____

11) Your shift is over and you're in a hurry to stop at the grocery store, get home, and prepare dinner before your guests arrive. On your way out of the building, you pass an elderly woman whom you saw visiting one of your patients earlier that afternoon. She left her headlights on when she parked her car, and now her battery is dead and her car won't start.

_____
_____
_____
_____
_____
_____
_____
_____

12) A doctor walks in the room and mistakes you for a nurse. He asks you to change the patient's catheter. As a new patient care technician, you haven't been trained on the procedure yet but you have read about it in your textbook.

_____
_____
_____
_____
_____
_____
_____
_____

✐ REVIEW QUESTIONS

Answer each of the following.

1) Discuss interdependence among health care workers and explain why it's important.

_____
_____
_____
_____
_____

_____

_____

2) List five factors that support strong interpersonal relationships among coworkers.

_____

_____

_____

_____

_____

_____

_____

_____

3) List five ways you can get to know your coworkers better to improve teamwork and interpersonal relationships.

_____

_____

_____

_____

_____

_____

_____

_____

4) Why are coworkers viewed as customers? Give three other examples of health care customers.

_____

_____

_____

_____

_____

_____

_____

5) Who are colleagues?

_____

_____

_____

_____

_____

_____

_____

6) Describe what it means to be loyal to your coworkers and to your employer. Give an example of each.

_____
_____
_____
_____
_____
_____
_____
_____

7) What are self-esteem and self-worth? What impact do you have on someone else's self-esteem and self-worth?

_____
_____
_____
_____
_____
_____
_____
_____

8) What are cliques? Why is it best to be inclusive?

_____
_____
_____
_____
_____
_____
_____

9) State "the golden rule" and describe why it's important in relationships.

_____
_____
_____
_____
_____
_____

10) What is synergy? How does it apply to relationships at work?

_____
_____

_____
_____
_____
_____
_____
_____

11) What is consensus? What makes it different from majority rules? Why is consensus important?

_____
_____
_____
_____
_____
_____
_____

12) What are group norms and why are they important? Give three examples.

_____
_____
_____
_____
_____
_____
_____

13) What is a multiskilled worker? Give two examples. List two benefits of employing multiskilled workers.

_____
_____
_____
_____
_____
_____
_____

14) Define _diversity_ and list five examples of cultural differences.

_____
_____
_____
_____

_____
_____
_____

15) Why is it important to find "common ground" among health care workers?

_____
_____
_____
_____
_____
_____
_____
_____

16) What are manners and why are they important in the workplace?

_____
_____
_____
_____
_____
_____
_____
_____

17) List five examples of good manners.

_____
_____
_____
_____
_____
_____
_____
_____

18) Explain why communication skills are the basis for effective relationships.

_____
_____
_____
_____
_____
_____
_____

19) What is conflict resolution and why is it important?

_____

_____

_____

_____

_____

_____

_____

_____

20) List four communication styles. Which one is most effective in conflict resolution and why?

_____

_____

_____

_____

_____

_____

_____

_____

21) What is a win-win resolution and why is it important?

_____

_____

_____

_____

_____

_____

_____

22) List five examples of good customer service.

_____

_____

_____

_____

_____

_____

(Answers to Review Questions are at the end of the book.)

Chapter Four

Personal Skills and the Health Care Professional

CHAPTER OBJECTIVES

Having completed this chapter, students will be able to:

✔ Define *personal skills,* and explain how they affect success as a health care worker.

✔ Define *personal image,* and describe how a health care worker's personal image affects the patients he or she serves.

✔ List several appearance and grooming traits that support an *un*professional image.

✔ List several examples of annoying and troublesome "personal habits."

✔ Describe how grammar and vocabulary impact their professional image.

✔ Discuss the importance of maintaining professionalism after hours.

✔ Define *personal management skills* and give several examples.

✔ Explain the importance of good time management skills, personal financial management skills, and stress management skills.

✔ List several techniques to improve time management, personal financial management, and stress management.

✔ Describe the importance of critical-thinking and problem-solving skills.

✔ List the steps involved in problem solving.

✔ Define *adaptive skills,* and explain why the ability to manage change is so important in health care today.

In previous chapters, we've discussed how professionalism brings together who you are as a person and how you contribute those traits in the workplace. We've covered reliability, commitment, character, morals, and how you work with and treat other people. Now it's time to explore the connection between your *personal* life and your *professional* life. Because you're only *one* person, it stands to reason that, if your personal life is out of control, your professional life is going to suffer, too. When you have good **personal skills,** your personal affairs are in order. This frees you up to concentrate on your job and your career. Of course, many of your personal skills transfer to the workplace and influence your reputation as a health care professional. This includes your personal image; your ability to manage time, finances, stress, and change; and your critical-thinking and problem-solving skills.

What does it take to have a well-orchestrated personal life that puts *you* on the right path to success in your career? Let's examine some personal skills and the impact they have on professionalism and success in the health care workplace.

Personal Image

One of the first things people notice about you is your **personal image**—the total impression you make on other people. Personal image includes your appearance, grooming, and posture; personal habits; and the grammar and language you use. What kind of an impression do *you* make on people? Are you neat, clean, and **well groomed?** When you come to work, are you dressed properly to perform the duties of your job? Do your appearance and posture convey pride, competence, and professionalism? Do any personal habits detract from your image? How about your **grammar** or the language you use?

Appearance and Grooming

Your personal image is especially important in patient care. Remember that patients need confidence in their caregivers. They want assurance that the people caring for them are competent and professional. How would *you* feel if *your* caregiver had a ripped uniform, dirty shoes, oily hair, grimy fingernails, or body odor? Would you wonder if that person's unprofessional appearance might also indicate a lack of competence in his or her work?

Other people besides patients are affected by your personal appearance, too. Family members and friends who visit patients also need reassurance that their loved ones are being cared for by professionals. Vendors, guests, and other people who come into your workplace expect to see employees supporting a professional environment. Your coworkers and supervisor expect you to uphold the company's professional standards, too.

Then there's you. When you *look* good, you *feel* good. Setting high standards for your personal appearance not only conveys an image of professionalism to others, it reinforces your pride and self-esteem. How can you expect others to view you as a professional if you don't look like or feel like a professional yourself?

Most employers have a written **dress code** outlining appropriate and inappropriate attire. Sometimes dress code requirements will vary from department to department depending on the duties involved. For example, maintenance workers would have a different dress code than departmental secretaries. Be sure you're familiar with the dress code for your job and do your best to uphold it.

Consider the following as a general "rule of thumb." If you don't wear a uniform, select clothing that's appropriate for the duties of your job. Clothes should be clean, pressed, and fit properly. Avoid clothing that is too short, too tight, or too revealing. Shoes should be clean, polished, and worn with socks or stockings. Keep makeup, jewelry, and other accessories to a minimum and in good taste. Earrings should not dangle or get in the way of doing your job. Long hair should be pulled back and secured to avoid sanitary or safety problems. Avoid wearing perfume or aftershave. (Strong aromas may not be welcome among patients and workers, and might aggravate breathing difficulties.) Sit up straight, stand erect, and don't slouch.

Remember, you don't come to work to set new fashion trends or win a beauty contest. Your clothing and accessories should support getting your work done efficiently and safely while instilling a feeling of confidence among those you serve.

Save your evening wear, party attire, sportswear, and the latest fashions for after hours. Tight pants, tank tops, miniskirts, bare midriffs, or low necklines are never acceptable. Even if your employer allows "casual days," remember that you're still in the workplace. If your job involves contact with patients and other customers, avoid wearing blue jeans or T-shirts.

Professionals are sensitive to cultural differences. Think twice about attire, accessories, or other aspects of personal appearance that might make someone else feel uncomfortable—such as nose rings, pierced tongues and lips, neon hair, spiked haircuts, tattoos, and extra-long fingernails.

Although it's a sensitive issue, one's weight needs to be mentioned briefly. People who are extremely overweight may notice an adverse affect on job opportunities. It's not unusual to hear a manager say, "He would not be considered for this job because the space he would have to work in is too cramped and confining for him to function properly." Although we would like to believe that body weight is not a factor in employment decisions, it happens. In surgery, for example, there may be concerns about an obese worker contaminating a sterile field in a cramped environment. In radiology, equipment controls may be housed in cubicles too confining for a large person. In jobs requiring heavy lifting or frequent physical activity, employers may feel that such activities could jeopardize the health and safety of an overweight worker. Although it's unfortunate that a person's body weight could have a negative impact on his or her career, it *is* a fact of life. If you are seriously overweight and wish to do something about it, work closely with your family physician to plan a safe and healthy course of action. If you are content with your weight, or for medical reasons are unable to reduce your weight, be on the lookout for employment opportunities where weight is not a factor.

Personal Habits

Personal habits are also part of your image and sometimes they can be annoying or troublesome to those around you. For example, don't wear noisy shoes or jewelry that jangles. Don't chew gum, pop your knuckles, bite your fingernails, or play childish pranks on coworkers. Avoid eating or drinking in view of patients and visitors. If you have difficulty hearing well, get fitted for a hearing aid. Asking people to repeat everything they say to you can become very annoying. Don't interrupt people when they're talking, and avoid completing sentences for someone else!

In many workplaces today, smoking cigarettes, cigars, and pipes has become taboo since increasing numbers of companies have gone smoke-free. If employees must smoke, they often must do so outside the building, huddled together on sidewalks, presenting a not-so-professional image to the public driving by. Some employers now hire only nonsmokers, and others offer employee smoking cessation classes at no charge.

If you smoke and your workplace has not yet gone smoke-free, always be considerate of those around you and ask before you light up. Better yet, head outside to protect other people from harmful secondhand smoke. If your workplace has gone smoke-free, accept the inconvenience but be careful. If your smoke breaks become too frequent or last too long, your absence from your work site could become a performance issue. If you smoke and wish to quit, join a support group and get your physician's advice.

Language and Grammar

The language you use can also reflect personal habits that other people might find annoying. For example, unless you're talking with your spouse or significant other, don't refer to people has "honey," "sweetie," or "dear." Adult females are "women" or "ladies," not "girls." Adult males are "men" not "boys." Some language is totally unacceptable in the workplace, such as obscenities, sexually explicit or risqué comments, and terms that demean members of any racial, cultural, or ethnic group. Language that might be acceptable after hours with your family or friends may be viewed as objectionable by coworkers, patients, or visitors. Telling jokes in poor taste and making "off-color" remarks is a bad idea, even during breaks. Remember the prior discussion about sexual harassment and creating an uncomfortable work environment for others. Even if you mean no harm, someone else's perception might be different. Always be respectful of other people's points of view and avoid using language they might not appreciate.

Grammar is an important part of your personal and professional image, too. Poor grammar is a warning signal, indicating a lack of education and refinement. Avoid mismatching the subject and verb in a sentence. For example, "We was there" should be "We *were* there." Or, "I seen you do that" should be "I *saw* you do that." "Me and him" should be "He and I." "It don't matter" should be "It *doesn't* matter." Poor grammar is learned and then reinforced by the people we are around frequently. If people close to you use incorrect grammar, it's likely you will, too. Just being aware of the need for good grammar might help. If your grammar is weak, work toward improving it. You might be surprised how much it can affect your personal and professional image.

First impressions are important—you might have only one opportunity to make a favorable impression on someone. In fact, *every* impression you make is important. As discussed earlier, to patients and other customers, you *are* the company you work for. Put together a total personal package that portrays a professional image. It's a big part of your job, and it can make or break your reputation as a professional.

Maintaining Professionalism after Hours

At first glance, you might not realize that, even when you're at home after work hours, some of your actions can affect your professional image. For example, how do you answer your telephone at home? What kind of impression does the recorded message on your home answering machine make on people who call you? Don't assume that every caller is a friend, a family member, or a stranger trying to sell you something. What if your supervisor calls, or a potential employer? Your home answering machine is an extension of your personal image so think about who might be calling you and the impression you want to make on them. If you allow your children to answer your telephone at home, teach them proper telephone manners and make sure they can take an accurate message for you.

Your relationships, both at work and outside of work, can have a positive or negative effect on your personal and professional image, too. The types of people with whom you associate are a reflection of who you are as a person. Look for people who can have a positive impact on your life. Avoid those who can get you into trouble and ruin your reputation.

It's a small world. You never know when you might run into your supervisor, a coworker, or someone who knows someone you know after hours. "So what?" you might ask. "If I'm not at work, what difference does it make?" In fact, it can make a great deal of difference! Your reputation goes with you *every place* you go. You never know who might be sitting across the room from you in a restaurant, bar, or some other public place. If you've had a few drinks and your voice gets loud, spreading gossip, revealing confidential information, or criticizing your employer can all come back to "haunt" you. If you call in sick when you really aren't and then go out in public, you never know whom you might encounter. If someone sees you and word gets back to your supervisor, you wouldn't be the first person to get fired from a job under circumstances like these.

If your work group, department, or company has a special event after hours, the standards that govern acceptable behavior at work apply during those events, too. Just because you're with coworkers outside the work setting doesn't mean the rules for professional behavior have changed. Conduct yourself in a professional manner. Don't overdrink, engage in wild behavior, and then regret it the next day. It's hard to reestablish trust, respect, and your professional reputation after making some poor decisions the night before.

Give serious thought to the pros and cons of dating someone you work with before you decide to do it. How might this different type of relationship affect both of you at work? What might happen if and when the relationship ends? Is it possible this person might end up being your boss someday or your subordinate? Sound advice is never to date your boss or someone who reports to you. It can lead to trouble and you may have to change jobs if things go sour.

The point of this discussion is that you are only one person. You aren't one person at work and a different person after work, so do your best to maintain a positive image after hours, too. It's OK to "let your hair down" and have a good time, but don't let your guard down, too. Always think before you act.

PERSONAL MANAGEMENT SKILLS

Personal management skills help determine how well you manage your personal lifestyle. Having your personal life in order helps support your success at work. Attendance and punctuality are good examples of how your personal life can affect your job. After all, does it really matter how professional you look or how competent you are if you can't get to work on time and be there when you're supposed to be? Your ability to show up for work on a daily basis and keep your appointments are some of the most important aspects of your job. If you have trouble managing your time, handling your finances, dealing with stress, or adapting to change, your personal life could have a negative impact on your job and your career. Let's take a closer look.

Time Management

When it seems like there are never enough hours in the day to get everything done that needs to get done, **time management** skills can be a big help. How well do *you* manage *your* time? Do you allow enough travel time to get from one place to another? Do you avoid booking yourself to be in two places at once? Are you sufficiently organized to get things done in a reasonable amount of time? Do you plan ahead for when your car might break down, the bus might be late, or your child or spouse might get sick? How well do you allocate your time to balance work, family, and other priorities in your life? Can you keep things organized at home and still hold down a job? Can you maintain your family and work obligations and still find time to enroll in a course or work toward another goal?

If managing time is a problem for you, consider some of the following suggestions. Always carry a pocket-sized calendar to record your work schedule and the dates, times, and places of appointments, meetings, classes, family and social activities, and other important events. Refer to your calendar every day and think about what's coming up tomorrow. Allow plenty of time to get from one activity to the next and plan ahead for the unexpected. Always anticipate that things might take longer than you had hoped. If traffic is heavy in the morning, if you might have trouble finding a parking place, or if bad weather could slow you down, schedule some extra travel time to avoid being late for work or an appointment. If the public transportation system is unreliable, have a plan for days when the bus is running late. If you ride to work with someone else, have a plan for when emergencies arise. If you have a personal doctor's appointment, allow some extra time in case the doctor is running late. If you have children, plan ahead for when they get sick or when your baby-sitter or child-care provider is not available at the last minute. Scheduling things too closely together and then encountering unexpected delays can put you behind schedule for the rest of the day.

Don't procrastinate! If something needs to be done, schedule time to do it and get it over with. Letting things build up is a sure way to become overwhelmed and disorganized. Effective organizational skills are vital in time management. Look for ways to become more productive and efficient. If you have a lot of paperwork to manage or records to maintain, have a good filing system so you can put things away and then find them quickly when you need them. Avoid becoming snowed under by huge projects. Break them down into smaller pieces and tackle one step at a time. Make written lists of things that need to be done, rank each item according to its priority, and then check things off as you complete them. When a task requires concentration, find a quiet place to work that's free of interruptions. Sometimes this might mean going to the public library or working at home after everyone else has gone to sleep. If you become overwhelmed with responsibilities, decide which are the most important and which you can let go. Eliminate activities that waste time and learn to say "No" when you're overbooked.

Most everyone is limited on how much paid sick leave and vacation time he or she gets as part of the job. Wise use of your paid time off is a crucial part of your overall time management strategy. If you use your sick time when you really aren't sick, what will happen if you *do* get sick and have no paid time off to cover your absence? We've already discussed the fact that professionals don't come to work sick and spread their germs to everyone around them. So if you must stay home to recover from an illness but you've already used up all of your sick time, can you afford to be off work with no pay? And if you're off sick but have no sick time to cover it, could your absence soon become a performance issue that might cost you your job? The best way to avoid these kinds of situations is to use your sick time wisely. Remember—plan ahead and expect the unexpected. Save your sick time for when you really need it, and use your vacation time for the other days you want to be off from work. As will soon be discussed, managing your vacation time wisely is important, too.

It goes without saying that your job should be a top priority in your life and in your personal schedule. But your family must be a top priority, too. Always keep in mind what's most important, and plan your schedule around your priorities. You can't create more hours in the day, but you can seize control of the time you have. After all, time is one of your most precious and most limited commodities. Learning how to manage it appropriately can have a huge impact on your personal and professional life.

Personal Financial Management

Managing another precious and limited commodity—your personal finances—can also have a major impact on your personal image and on your reputation as a professional. How effective are your **personal financial management** skills? Are your personal finances under control? Do you overspend and rely on credit cards with high interest rates? Do you have trouble paying your bills on time? Are you behind in repaying loans? Is there a chance a creditor might call you or your employer at work, or send a tow truck to the parking lot to repossess your car? Could personal financial problems cause you embarrassment at work?

Professionals have their personal finances in order. This doesn't mean they're wealthy—they've just learned to live within their means and practice good financial planning. It's important to develop a budget, monitor and control your expenses, and make the most of your limited financial resources. Keep your checking account balanced, and maintain accurate records of how much money you have coming in and going out each month. Match up paydays with the dates you pay your bills, to avoid having to pay extra fees because your payments were late. Some of the best advice anyone can follow for sound financial management is to hold off buying something until you have the money to pay for it. Avoid the temptation to buy things on credit—especially items you don't absolutely need. In most cases, one major credit card should be sufficient. Use that card only for emergencies or to make purchases that you already have the cash to cover. When your monthly bill arrives, pay the balance in full. If you cannot pay the balance in full, make sure your credit card has the lowest interest rate and annual fee available. In addition to paying the interest that's due each month, always pay something to help lower the balance, too. If you're already in debt due to using your credit cards too often, work with a financial counselor to pay off your debts and then *stop* using your cards. If you possess several credit cards, either discontinue all but one, or put the extra cards away someplace where you won't be tempted to use them. If you do decide to keep your extra cards, remember that you may still be subject to annual fees to keep each card current. Excess credit cards may also affect your credit rating because they may be viewed as "potential" debt.

Sound financial planning applies to other kinds of credit purchases too, such as automobile and home loans. Before you buy a car, think about your monthly income and other expenses. How much you can actually afford for a car payment? What about car insurance, license plates, gasoline, maintenance, and parking expenses? When applying for a loan to purchase a home, ask yourself how much can you afford as a house payment each month. What about home insurance, property taxes, and termite inspections? What might happen when your furnace breaks down or the living room carpet needs to be replaced? Millions of Americans have become overwhelmed with credit and loan debts, everyday living expenses, and unexpected repair bills. Serious financial problems can occur quickly and easily, yet it can take years to dig yourself out of a deep financial hole. Thinking about sound financial decisions in advance can keep this from happening to you.

Even if you have little money left after paying your bills each month, it's still important to have a savings plan and to stick with it. A savings account can help you cover unexpected expenses and put some funds away for the future. One of the best ways to save money is through a payroll deduction plan where you work. Money is taken out of your paycheck before you receive it, and deposited into an interest-earning savings account. Even if the amount is small, you'll be surprised how quickly the balance can grow. The same is true for investments. A small amount of money deducted from your paycheck and invested wisely into stocks or bonds can reap significant rewards years from now. Also, even if you're young, think about investing some money in a retirement fund. These types of investments may be exempt from income tax until you withdraw the money years from now, and when you get close to retirement you'll be glad you took the time to plan ahead. The same is true if you're planning to go back to school someday to continue your education, or if you must finance the education of your children or other loved ones. College is expensive, and it's never too soon to start saving and planning ahead.

Don't forget the need for insurance. How much and what types of insurance are required to protect yourself and your family from accidents and catastrophic events? It's easy to ignore the need for insurance and to spend that money on something else. But if you own a car, a home, or other personal assets, you should protect your investments with an adequate amount of insurance. Consider the need for life insurance and how much health insurance is adequate to protect yourself and your loved ones. If you have insurance benefits at work, make sure you're familiar with them and using them to the fullest potential. If not, get some counseling from an insurance agent you can trust.

Set priorities for how to allocate your limited financial resources and then make your financial decisions accordingly. Sometimes it's better to buy a used car rather than a new car, or to buy a smaller home rather than a larger home, if the extra money is needed for savings, adequate insurance coverage, or planning for your future. Think twice before loaning money or cosigning for a loan for friends, relatives, or coworkers. Can you get by without that money if the loan is never repaid? If you must loan money, make sure you have a written, signed agreement detailing plans for repayment.

Stress Management

Having to make financial decisions can be a source of stress in your life, but there are many other stress-related factors too, not the least of which is working in health care. In fact, jobs in health care are among the most stress-producing occupations in the United States. Many health care workers function under a great deal of pressure. Jobs may involve lots of responsibility, physical and mental exertion, the need to respond quickly, and the challenge of interacting with diverse groups of people who are under a lot of stress themselves. Effective **stress management** skills can be quite valuable in both your personal life and at work. Your ability to manage stress is also a key factor in your personal image as a professional. If you "blow up," "melt down," or run for the door at the first sign of stress, you may be letting your coworkers and your patients down. Your ability to perform the duties of your job may be affected, and your personal health and wellness may suffer. Good stress management techniques can help you keep everything in balance and add more enjoyment to your life.

In order to manage stress, you must be able to (1) recognize *when* stress is affecting you, (2) understand *how* and *why* stress is affecting you, and (3) identify *where* the stress is coming from before you can take action to alleviate your stress. For example, maybe you felt some stress yesterday afternoon when your supervisor called you into her office. Think back to that situation and examine it more closely. Did you feel stress any other time yesterday afternoon, or only when you got called into your supervisor's office? Did you experience that same feeling when she called you into her office last week too, or only yesterday afternoon? Exactly *when* is the stress experienced? Then think about *how* the stress is affecting you. Does it make you feel anxious, nervous, or worried? Do you feel as if something bad is about to happen to you? Then ask yourself *why*. Why does getting called into your supervisor's office cause you to feel stress? What happened the last time you got called in, or what did you hear happened to someone else who got called in? Asking yourself questions like these can help you figure out *where* the stress is coming from. Unless you can identify the source of your stress, it can be difficult to deal with it or eliminate the stress altogether. Maybe you made a mistake on a patient's chart, forgot to clock in this morning, or had a disagreement with a coworker. Maybe your supervisor has found out and wants to discuss the matter with you. Or maybe a week ago you got called in because of poor attendance, and you know your supervisor has been watching you closely. Getting called into her office again could mean corrective action or getting fired from your job. In any case, the important thing is to know when you're affected by stress, how and why it's affecting you, and where it's coming from so you can decide what to do about the situation. Once you've identified the source of your stress, you can sometimes totally eliminate it. For example, if you know getting called into your supervisor's office can be a stressful situation for you, make sure your attendance, work performance, and interpersonal skills are all good. Then when you get called in the next time, maybe you'll be more optimistic. After all, perhaps your supervisor wants to pass on a letter she received from a patient, acknowledging how much he appreciated the extra kindness you showed him during his last stay at the hospital. Or maybe she wants to invite you to participate on a new committee or help with an upcoming project.

Obviously, there are many other sources of stress besides concerns about your supervisor. Maybe you get stressed out when you have to rush. Would better organizational and time management skills prevent you from having to rush so often? Maybe just the thought of having to get up in front of your coworkers next week to give a report makes you break out in a cold sweat. Would practicing in front of family members or friends first help? Maybe having to take a test for a course you're enrolled in has your stomach tied up in knots. Did you spend enough time studying and preparing for the test? Maybe being verbally attacked by an angry customer increases your blood pressure and makes you want to explode. Would some additional conflict resolution skills help? Just knowing where your stress is coming from can help you decide how to deal with it better.

Not all stress can be anticipated or eliminated and this is especially true when working in the health care environment. You don't always know what's going to happen next, and sometimes things can catch you off guard. Maybe a piece of equipment has malfunctioned with no warning, a coworker has called in sick on an unusually busy morning, a new coworker has shown up on your unit with no advance notice, or one of your patients has gone into cardiac arrest suddenly. At times like these, when you're under a great deal of stress, you must stay focused on your job and deal with the situation to the very best of your ability. Then, when the day is over, you need an outlet for your stress. It helps to have someone you can talk with—a person who can relate to what you've experienced and help you think through it. Getting emotional support is especially important for people who work directly with patients. The stress of working with sick and injured people every day can take a toll on the mental health of caregivers. If your job involves this type of stress, or other kinds of stress that wear you down physically, mentally, or emotionally, be sure to seek out professional help when you need it. Your employer may have counselors on staff, or chaplains, human resource personnel, or other people who can help when stress becomes too much for you to handle on your own.

Stress can affect your physical health as well as your mental and emotional health. Many physicians and researchers are convinced that stress is a contributing factor to several different diseases and abnormalities. Stress can make you sick and cause symptoms such as headaches, fatigue, sleep problems, diarrhea, indigestion, ulcers, hypertension, dizziness, hives, grinding teeth, skin disorders, and stuttering.

Stress has been linked with heart attacks, high blood pressure, alcoholism, depression, and drug abuse. People with "Type A" personalities are among the most susceptible to stress-related disorders. They are highly competitive, impatient, high achievers with strong perfectionist tendencies. They often rush from place to place, work long hours, have an intense drive to get things done, become frustrated easily, and have trouble relaxing. When Type A personalities have a lifestyle that includes smoking, drinking, a poor diet, a lack of exercise, and being overweight, they become targets for stress-related illness. If you're a Type A personality yourself, or if the stress you experience tends to affect your health in any way, don't wait until it's too late. Watch for the warning signs—those personal signals that stress is affecting you—and then seek help in dealing with it.

Stress in your personal life can impact your job, just as stress at work can impact your personal life. Keeping things in balance is the key. Try to keep your stress at work from affecting your home life and your relationships with family and friends. Try to keep stress in your personal life, such as marital problems and financial difficulties, from affecting your work. That's easier said than done because, as has been mentioned previously, you are only one person. Keep in mind that *any change* in your life can be stressful. This includes the death of a spouse or other loved one, divorce, personal injury, or getting fired from your job. Even changes that you perceive as good can produce stress, such as getting married, having a baby, moving into a new home, getting a new job, and graduating from school. Closing on a home mortgage, having a son or daughter move away from home, changing your work schedule, and Christmas can all be stress producing. Whenever possible, try to limit the number of stress-producing factors in your life at any given time. For example, try to avoid changing jobs and getting married at the same time, or having a baby and moving into a new home. If you're returning to school while continuing to work, avoid changing jobs if possible or starting a family. The more you can avoid or manage stress-producing factors, the less the likelihood of your suffering any stress-related problems.

Learn to relax and schedule time for recreation, hobbies, sports, and other personal interests. Maintain a healthy balance between work and play. As mentioned earlier, use your vacation time wisely. All workers need time off to rejuvenate themselves and feel refreshed. Get plenty of sleep and exercise, eat properly, and avoid short-term escapes like alcohol and other drugs, and smoking. Use your time management skills to help you slow down when you can and stop putting pressure on yourself unnecessarily. Strengthen your interpersonal communication and conflict resolution skills, and don't keep negative feelings bottled up inside you.

An important part of managing stress is being happy and well adjusted. Professionals like themselves. They have high levels of self-esteem and self-respect. They have a positive self-image and know they are worthy individuals. It's difficult for others to have confidence in you if you don't have confidence in yourself. Look for the good in yourself. Be patient with yourself and with others. Know your limits and work within them. Avoid being a perfectionist—no one is perfect. Setting unrealistic goals is counterproductive and leads only to disappointment, low self-esteem, and unnecessary stress. Set high but realistic standards for yourself and feel good about your accomplishments.

Strive to enrich yourself. Recognize your potential, learn all you can, and constantly reach for new heights. You have the ability to reach your goals and to excel in your work and in your personal life, if you learn to manage your stress and not let it rule you.

Problem Solving and Critical Thinking

One of the best stress management tools is good **problem-solving** skills. Every day we're faced with a variety of problems to solve, both in our personal lives and at work. By using **critical-thinking** skills and a systematic approach to addressing problems, you can usually come up with a solution that will work. You must be able to (1) identify a problem when you see one, (2) define what the problem is, (3) gather information to learn more about the problem, (4) identify possible solutions, and (5) decide which solution is the best.

When faced with a problem, take it one step at a time. What exactly is the problem? It's very important to answer this question before moving on to solutions; otherwise, you might be focusing on the wrong problem. For example, perhaps you've noticed that a coworker in your work group named John isn't doing his share of the work. It seems as if every time things get busy, John's gone someplace or he's down the hall helping another work group. It's become a problem because his lack of help is slowing things down and preventing you from getting your work done on time. What should you do to solve this problem? Round up your coworkers and everyone confront John? Report him to his supervisor?

First, figure out *exactly* what is the problem. Is John lazy? Does he have an "I don't care" attitude about his job? Does he disappear on purpose, leaving his coworkers to finish up without him? Doesn't he care about his patients? Before you can solve this problem, you need to gather more information. Does John always avoid helping with the work or just at certain times? Is it all types of work he avoids or just certain tasks? When he's gone from his work area, where does he go and what does he do? When he's down the hall with another work group, why is he there and what is he doing? Does it matter if his supervisor is in the area or not?

Upon further investigation, you realize that each time a patient must be moved from his or her bed over to a cart, John is gone from the area. When this happens, you must go find someone else who's available to help lift and move the patient. Because everyone is busy, it takes at least fifteen minutes to round up help and get the patient moved. With several patients having to be moved each day, over the course of your shift you get farther and farther behind in your schedule. Now that you think about it, coworkers are starting to get angry with you because you're pulling them away from their work. The staff in the radiology and physical therapy departments are beginning to complain because your patients are arriving late for their tests and treatments, delaying the schedules in those departments, too. So, if John's not around when it's time to move patients, where is he and what is he doing?

Further investigation shows that John is not just disappearing or lounging in the break room. In fact, he's keeping very busy. He's helping the unit down the hall rearrange its stockroom to use the same organizational system that your unit just set up. He's also delivering requisitions to the clinical lab and picking up patient charts from the medical records department. He isn't lazy, he doesn't have an "I don't care" attitude about his job, and he does care about patients.

Before long, it becomes obvious that the *only* time John is gone from his work area is when there's a patient to be moved. Having identified the *specific* problem puts you in a much better position to solve it. Instead of accusing John of laziness, reporting him to his supervisor, or labeling him as inconsiderate, you can find out why John disappears when there's a patient to be moved and hopefully work with him to solve the problem. Using your assertive communication skills, you can tell John that his absence during times when patients need to be moved is causing delays. You can tell him you appreciate the fact that he's off helping another unit or doing tasks to help your unit, but when there are patients to be moved, you need help moving them. You've given John the benefit of the doubt, you've explained why his absence is causing problems, and you've done so in a manner that shows your respect for him as a coworker. You may find out that John has hurt his back. He's avoided telling anyone because he knows that lifting and moving patients, equipment, and supplies is part of his job. He might be concerned that, if he can't perform his job adequately, he could get in trouble with his supervisor or even lose his job. So he just disappears at the right time but stays busy still helping out his own unit and other units, too. Now that you know the exact problem and its cause, you and John can work together to solve it.

When faced with a problem, avoid jumping to conclusions. As mentioned above, identify and clarify the problem. Gather as much information as you can and then examine the evidence you've found. Decide what options are available to solve the problem and which option would work best. Implement your solution and evaluate the results. In the case of John's disappearance, using your critical-thinking skills and taking a step-by-step approach to the situation, you were able to solve the problem while maintaining a positive relationship with a coworker. There's almost always a good solution to every problem, but you may have to invest some time and energy to find it.

Effective problem-solving and critical-thinking skills are mandatory for a well-orchestrated personal and professional life. The more you use your critical-thinking skills, the better they will get. Working in health care provides lots of opportunities for problem solving, not the least of which is dealing with the many changes that present themselves.

Managing Change

In today's health care workplace, one of the most important personal skills is the ability to manage change. Just when you think everything is arranged as it should be, something changes. For example, your job might need to be redesigned to fit within a restructured department. You might be given some new responsibilities or be cross-trained to perform some additional functions. You might be reassigned to a different work group or get a new supervisor. Policies and procedures might change, or your work schedule might get adjusted. A new member might join your work team or you might be transferred to a different team. The company you work for might merge with another company, or your employer might move to a new location.

At the same time you're affected by change at work, you probably also face changes in your personal life. Family responsibilities, relationships with friends, and pressures involving finances, housing, transportation, and health all cause many changes over the course of our lives. How well do you deal with change? How effective are your **adaptive skills?** Do you resist change or are you flexible, versatile, and adaptive? It's almost impossible to avoid change. If you are the type of person who resists change, you're going to face some very difficult challenges. On the other hand, if you're flexible, versatile, and adaptive, you're well prepared for the many changes life will throw your way.

Years ago, health care workers were encouraged to learn to *cope* with change. Then, when the pace of change increased, everyone was encouraged to learn to *manage* change. Now, because things change so rapidly in health care, workers must *embrace* change and even *lead* change at times. Successful health care professionals will tell you that change can be a positive influence in your life if you learn to accept it and let it open new doors for you. Having your job redesigned can be pretty scary. You might have to learn some new skills and take on some new responsibilities. But the more new challenges you face, the more you grow. And the more you grow, the better your chances for advancement. View change as positive and learn to make it work *for* you instead of *against* you. After all, do you really want your personal life and your career to be exactly the same five years from now as it is today? Advancing in your career is a vital part of being a health care professional. Do you have a well thought out plan for your future and how you're going to get there? Are you committed to working hard to achieve your goals? These are topics for the next chapter.

GLOSSARY OF TERMS

personal skills   the ability to manage aspects of your life outside of work

personal image   the total impression created by a person

well groomed   clean and neat

grammar   system of word structures and arrangements

dress code   standards for attire and appearance

personal management skills   the ability to manage time, finances, stress, and change

time management   the ability to organize and allocate one's time to increase productivity

personal financial management   the ability to make sound decisions about personal finances

stress management   the ability to deal with stress and overcome stressful situations

problem solving   using a systematic process to solve problems

critical thinking   using careful analysis and objective judgment

adaptive skills   the ability to adjust to change

EXERCISES

Complete the following.

1) How would someone who knows you well describe your "personal image"?

_____

_____

_____

_____

_____

_____

2) Describe a personal experience to illustrate "When you look good you feel good."

_____

_____

_____

_____

_____

_____

_____

3) Identify someone you've observed with a poor personal image. What factors contributed to that image? What improvements were needed to support a positive personal and professional image?

_____

_____

_____

_____

_____

_____

_____

4) Make a list of words that you've heard used in the workplace that are inappropriate.

_____

_____

_____

_____

_____

_____

_____

5) Make a list of ten common grammatical errors and indicate how to correct them.

_____

_____

_____

_____

_____

_____

6) Describe a situation that you've observed or experienced yourself where professionalism was not maintained after hours. What effect did this have on the person's professional reputation?

_____

_____

_____

_____

_____

_____

7) How would someone who knows you well describe your "personal management" skills?

_____

_____

_____

_____

_____

_____

8) Describe a personal situation where better time management skills would help you.

_____

_____

_____

_____

_____

_____

9) If you don't already have one, develop a personal budget. List three ways you could improve upon managing your personal finances.

_____

_____

_____

_____

_____

_____

10) List five sources of stress in your life and describe some of your own stress management techniques.

_____

_____

_____

_____

_____

_____

11) Describe your own "self-image" and what influences it.

_____

_____

_____

_____

_____

_____

12) Think back to a recent problem you faced. Describe the problem and the steps you took to solve it. Did your approach to problem solving work? Why or why not?

_____

_____

_____

_____

_____

13) Think back to a time when you have faced a major change in your personal life or in a job. Describe the change and how you responded to it. Was your response effective? Why or why not?

_____

_____

_____

_____

_____

SELF-ASSESSMENT

Think about yourself and how you approach your work. Consider each of the following and check all that apply.

_____ 1) My personal life supports my success as a health care professional.

_____ 2) My personal image makes a good first impression on the people I meet.

_____ 3) My personal appearance and grooming support my reputation as a health care professional.

_____ 4) I follow the dress code established by my employer or my school.

_____ 5) My clothes are neat, clean, and appropriate for my job.

_____ 6) I avoid personal habits that are annoying to others.

_____ 7) I concentrate on good grammar and avoid using inappropriate language in the workplace.

_____ 8) I recognize the importance of maintaining a professional image after hours.

_____ 9) I think before I act.

_____ 10) My personal management skills support my success at work or school.

_____ 11) I manage my time effectively.

_____ 12) I anticipate the unexpected, allow extra time, and arrive for my appointments on schedule.

_____ 13) I avoid procrastination and use good organizational skills to be productive and efficient.

_____ 14) I manage my sick leave, vacation time, and other time off from my job wisely.

_____ 15) My personal financial management skills are effective and my personal finances are under control.

_____ 16) I avoid the temptation to buy things on credit, especially things I don't really need.

_____ 17) I set priorities and allocate my financial resources wisely.

_____ 18) I know when stress is affecting me and I can identify the source of that stress.

_____ 19) Although I can't always anticipate or eliminate stress, I am usually effective in managing it.

_____ 20) I avoid letting stress affect my health.

_____ 21) I have good critical-thinking skills and am effective at solving problems.

_____ 22) I am flexible, versatile, and adaptive to change.

_____ 23) I seize opportunities that come with change and find ways to make change work *for* me instead of *against* me.

✍ INDIVIDUAL NEXT-STEP ACTION PLANS

Based on your Self-Assessment, complete the following:

1) My strongest skills are:

_____

_____

_____

_____

_____

_____

_____

2) My areas for improvement are:

_____

_____

_____
_____
_____
_____
_____

3) Five things I plan to do to improve my skills:

    a) _____

    b) _____

    c) _____

    d) _____

    e) _____

WHAT IF SCENARIOS

What would you do in the following situations?

    1) You're scheduled to work tomorrow but waited until the last minute to wash your uniforms. A friend calls to invite you to a movie, but you don't have time for both laundry chores and the movie, too.

_____
_____
_____
_____
_____
_____

    2) Your company's dress code allows denim jeans and T-shirts on Fridays for "casual day." Because you've been cross-trained to fill in for the customer service department when it is short-handed, it's possible you could be asked to work at the information desk in the main lobby with little or no notice.

_____
_____
_____
_____
_____
_____

3) You've spent six months working out at a fitness center and look really good in tight blouses and short skirts. Hopefully, the cute guy who started working in medical records last week will notice you and ask you out.

_____

_____

_____

_____

_____

_____

_____

4) Some of the employees you eat lunch with use crude language, and at times it can be overheard by other people in your company's cafeteria.

_____

_____

_____

_____

_____

_____

_____

5) The only free time you have to jog on a regular basis is during your lunch break. Your break is long enough to get some good exercise, but you don't have time to take a shower before resuming work.

_____

_____

_____

_____

_____

_____

_____

6) You and a group of coworkers decide to start meeting at a popular bar on Saturday nights to "let your hair down" and have a good time. On the very first night, one person in your group drinks too much and ends up in a fistfight with a stranger seated at the next table. You overhear the bartender calling the police.

_____

_____

_____

_____

_____

_____

7) It seems there are never enough hours in the day for you to get everything done that you want to do. You work full time, participate in two bowling leagues each week, transport your children to their sporting events, volunteer at a local golf course, belong to three different community organizations, and take two courses each semester toward the degree you've been working on. Last week, you were late for work twice, called in sick the day your son's school was closed because of the weather, and had to cancel a dentist appointment at the last minute. You know your job is important but so are your family, friends, and other activities.

_____

_____

_____

_____

_____

_____

8) You just received a pay raise, giving you an extra $25 in each paycheck. Then the telephone rang and you found out you qualified for a new credit card that you hadn't even applied for. With your pay raise and a $5,000 credit limit, you've got the money you need to buy that new home computer and television set your children have been begging you for.

_____

_____

_____

_____

_____

_____

9) For the past month, you've been having headaches and difficulty sleeping at night. You're less patient with your children and have yelled at them several times. Even though you've been eating more than usual, you seem to have very little energy and can't keep up with physical activities. Yesterday, when your supervisor asked you to work overtime, you blew up and said, "No! Why can't somebody else do it? Why does it always have to be me?"

_____

_____

_____

_____

_____

_____

10) Your job is a twenty-minute drive from your home and your car is no longer reliable. It has 105,000 miles on it and needs several repairs. Through payroll deductions, you've saved enough money for a year's worth of car insurance and a down payment on a new vehicle, but you aren't sure you can afford the loan payments every month.

_____
_____
_____
_____
_____
_____
_____

11) The company where you work has merged with another company and as a result several departments have been restructured. The job you've had for five years still exists and several new jobs have been created. You qualify to apply for one of the new jobs, but if you get it, you must satisfactorily complete three weeks of training. The pay for the new job is only slightly higher than your current pay. But, after a year of work experience in the new job, you'd be eligible for a promotion with even more pay.

_____
_____
_____
_____
_____
_____
_____

✍ REVIEW QUESTIONS

Answer each of the following.

1) What are "personal skills" and how do they affect success as a health care worker?

_____
_____
_____
_____

_____

_____

_____

2) List five personal appearance and grooming traits that support an *un*professional image.

_____

_____

_____

_____

_____

_____

3) Describe how a health care worker's personal image affects the patients he or she serves.

_____

_____

_____

_____

_____

_____

4) What is a dress code and why is it important?

_____

_____

_____

_____

_____

5) List three examples of personal habits that support an *un*professional image.

_____

_____

_____

_____

_____

6) Explain how grammar and vocabulary affect your image.

_____

_____

_____

_____

_____

_____

_____

7) Describe why is it important to maintain professionalism after hours.

_____

_____

_____

_____

_____

_____

_____

8) List three examples of personal management skills.

_____

_____

_____

_____

_____

_____

_____

9) Explain why time management skills are important, and list three time management strategies.

_____

_____

_____

_____

_____

_____

_____

10) Explain why personal financial management skills are important, and list three financial management strategies.

_____

_____

_____

_____

_____

_____

_____

11) List three examples of how stress can affect someone's health, and list three
strategies to help manage stress.

_____

_____

_____

_____

_____

_____

12) What is a positive self-image and why is it important?

_____

_____

_____

_____

_____

_____

13) Why are creative-thinking and problem-solving skills important?

_____

_____

_____

_____

_____

_____

14) List the steps involved in problem solving.

_____

_____

_____

_____

_____

_____

15) What are adaptive skills and why are they important in today's health care
workplace?

_____

_____

_____

_____

_____

_____

_____

_____

(Answers to Review Questions are at the end of the book.)

Chapter Five

Growth and Advancement

CHAPTER OBJECTIVES

Having completed this chapter, students will be able to:

- ✔ Explain the difference between a stagnant career and a dynamic career.
- ✔ List questions to ask themselves in career planning.
- ✔ List resources that can help with career planning and advancement.
- ✔ Describe "transferable skills" and how they apply in career planning.
- ✔ Differentiate between "aptitude" and "abilities."
- ✔ Explain the value of personal assessments.
- ✔ Define *basic skills* and explain why they're important.
- ✔ List ways to explore employment opportunities where they live.
- ✔ define *goals, short-term goals, long-term goals,* and *realistic goals,* and explain why goals are important.
- ✔ Discuss the value of role models and mentors.
- ✔ Identify the importance of computer training in career advancement.
- ✔ Explain why an application form is an important part of the selection process.
- ✔ List factors in completing and submitting an application form appropriately.
- ✔ Describe preemployment or preadmission testing and explain why it is done.
- ✔ List important factors in participating in an interview for a new job or for admission into a training program.
- ✔ Explain why it's important never to falsify or exaggerate information about themselves on an application form or during an interview.

As mentioned at the end of the previous chapter, it's important to keep an eye on where your career is headed and to make good decisions about your future. Health care professionals rarely stay **stagnant.** They're always looking for opportunities to learn new things, acquire new skills, accept new responsibilities, and grow personally and professionally. How much of your **potential** for growth and development has yet to be tapped?

Planning for your future, setting realistic goals, and hanging in there without giving up are important steps in a **dynamic** health career. Regardless of your age, don't hesitate to dream and always ask yourself, "What comes next in my personal life and in my career?" Keep an eye on your future, but don't forget to appreciate the "here and now," too. After all, life is a journey, not a destination. It's the adventure along the way that makes life worth living. *Plan* for tomorrow, but *live* for today. Enjoy each and every step along the way. Stop to "smell the roses," recognize your accomplishments, and learn from your mistakes.

CAREER PLANNING

Take stock of where you are now in your career and think about where you might be headed. What do you really like about your work and what would you change if you could? Have you noticed other jobs that appeal to you? Do you want to stay in the same line of work for several more years or think about trying something different? It's not unusual for people to change jobs several times during their careers. Sometimes, people switch to an entirely different occupation. Other times, they remain in the same occupation but apply their knowledge and skills in a different job or in a different setting. Think about your own **occupational preferences.** Maybe you're working in a hospital now but would like to explore job opportunities in an outpatient clinic or a doctor's office. Perhaps you're working in a department like housekeeping, nutrition and dietetics, or central supply and would like to have a job with more patient contact. Maybe you're working as a nurse or a nurse extender with one type of patients but would someday like to work with a different type of patients. Perhaps you work in maintenance but would like to learn more about engineering or skilled trades. Maybe you work in patient billing but want to progress into an administrative secretary position.

One of the best ways to help you decide in which direction to head is **job shadowing.** Observe workers in other jobs and in other kinds of employment settings to see what a typical day is like. Ask workers what they like most about their jobs and what advice they might offer you. Although it's easy to read about a certain type of career or job in a booklet or pamphlet, there's no substitute for actually *being there* and seeing firsthand all that is involved.

Having a variety of employment opportunities is one of the benefits of working in health care, and your **transferable skills** can usually be applied in different kinds of jobs. You can change jobs several times and still stay in the same occupational field, often working for the same organization. You might want to stay in the same discipline (nursing, environmental services, secretarial and clerical, diagnostics, etc.) but progress upward to a job with more responsibility (charge nurse, housekeeping supervisor, administrative secretary, chief technologist, etc.). You might want to make a lateral move into another discipline where your transferable skills can give you a head start (from a patient transportation escort to a physical therapy aide; from an inventory and stocking clerk to a surgery instrument technician; from a medical assistant to an inpatient medical coder, etc.). You might want to become **multiskilled**—cross-trained to provide multiple functions, often in more than one discipline (a nursing assistant cross-trained to perform phlebotomy, EKGs, and higher-level patient care functions; a radiographer cross-trained to perform ultrasound procedures; a maintenance worker cross-trained in biomedical equipment repair, etc.). Of course, there's always the option of taking the skills you've learned in health care and switching to a totally different occupational field, like education, the hotel or food industry, business, retail sales, or production and manufacturing.

When thinking about your career options, consider the following:

1. Occupational preferences (the kind of work and work setting you prefer)
2. Abilities and aptitude (your current knowledge and skills, plus your capacity to learn more)
3. Employment opportunities (the availability of good-paying jobs with opportunities for advancement close to where you live)

Personal Assessments and Basic Skills

One of the best ways to help you identify your occupational preferences, abilities, and aptitude is by taking some **personal assessments.** Guidance counselors and educational advisers have a wide variety of different assessments from which to choose, and they can help you decide which assessments would be most valuable in your career planning. Assessments are like insurance policies—they help ensure you're on the right track and adequately prepared to tackle the next step in your career.

It's important to plan ahead, take one step at a time, and avoid rushing into a situation for which you might not be prepared. For example, don't sign up for an educational program until you're sure you have the **basic skills** and the academic background you need to complete the program successfully. Once again, this is where personal assessments can help. Work with an educational adviser to have your basic skills (fundamental reading, language, and math) assessed. Strong basic skills are the foundation upon which you build new knowledge and skills. If your basic skills are weak and you don't shore them up before starting an educational program, you may struggle each step of the way and possibly fail to succeed. For example, if you're reading at a fifth-grade level and the textbooks for your educational program are written for high school graduates, you'll probably have difficulty comprehending the material. If your math skills are weak, you may have trouble learning more difficult math because you have not yet mastered basic math. The same is true of weak language skills posing a barrier to passing advanced courses in written and verbal communication. Don't take shortcuts in basic skills preparation. If an assessment identifies a weak area, shore it up before applying to a training program.

Exploring Employment Opportunities

As mentioned above, health care workers have many employment opportunities from which to choose. Before deciding on a career plan, be sure to identify job opportunities where you live. Investigate hospitals in your area, but don't forget also to look into outpatient facilities, home care agencies, community health clinics, physician practices, and public health organizations. Where are the best employment opportunities that match your interests and abilities? Get in the habit of reading the classified advertisements in local newspapers, and track job opportunities from week to week. Talk with other area health care workers to get their opinions on the best places to work. Meet with human resource personnel to investigate job openings, pay, benefits, and opportunities for growth. Ask a librarian to help you track down the latest information on what kinds of jobs are in demand and where. This is one time to really do your homework. Make sure that the type of job you're preparing for will lead to good employment opportunities in your part of the country.

Setting Goals

Once you've explored your occupational interests, completed the appropriate assessments, and identified employment opportunities in your part of the country, you're ready to set **goals** for the next phase of your career. Goals are well-defined stepping-stones that help you progress from where you are now to where you eventually want to be. Short-term goals are those attained in a relatively brief period of time—up to about two years—whereas long-term goals take much longer. Long-term goals often involve meeting several short-term goals along the way. For example, if your long-term goal is to graduate from nursing school, your short-term goals might include earning passing grades in some prerequisite courses, saving money for tuition and books, and lining up a part-time job to help with living expenses while you're a student. If your long-term goal is a job that pays enough to finance the purchase of a new home, your short-term goals might include learning some new skills, taking supervisor training, and passing a national certification exam in your field.

Although it's important to dream about your future and "stretch" to reach your potential, it's also important to set realistic, attainable goals that are right for you. **Role models** and **mentors** can help. Role models are people who already have the kind of abilities, education, job, and professional reputation that you aspire to achieve yourself. Obviously, you can learn a lot from a role model because that person has already attained the goals that you are setting out to accomplish. Get to know your role model, observe what makes him or her successful, and decide if the approach your role model took would also work for you. Working with a mentor can be a big help, too. Unlike role models, mentors have not necessarily achieved the same goals you hope to achieve. But mentors can provide you with insight, advice, and encouragement to help you each step of the way. (While on the subject of role models and mentors, it's important for *you* to serve as a role model and mentor for other people, too. Remember, we're all on this road together. Just as others are helping you meet your goals, you can help other people reach theirs.)

College Courses and Computer Training

If you haven't already done so, one of the first steps in your career plan might be to take some college courses. Having had your basic skills assessed to be sure you're ready for more advanced learning, consider taking just one college-level course to "get your feet wet" prior to applying for an entire educational program. This will give you the opportunity to see what college-level course work is like without having to take several courses at the same time. You'll also get into the habit of studying, taking tests, and completing course assignments on time. Once you've done well in your first course, enroll in another one. As your skills get stronger and your confidence grows, take more than one course at a time. This gradual approach to meeting short-term goals will set you up for success in the early stages of your career plan. If your long-term goal is to graduate from a **postsecondary** educational program, the grades you've earned along the way will help convince the admissions committee (and yourself!) that you have a high potential for completing the program successfully. If earning a college degree or a professional certification is your goal, arrange a meeting with an educational adviser to be sure your course work will apply toward requirements.

If postsecondary education is part of your career plan, and even if it isn't, consider gaining some basic computer skills. To function in today's world and to advance in your career, computer skills are no longer just an option—they're a necessity. Don't be afraid of computers. Once you've learned the basics, you'll be off and running, eager to learn even more. Acquiring computer skills is a great way to build confidence and self-esteem, and to keep up with your children!

Balancing Priorities and Career Advancement

As you set goals and proceed with your career plan, it's important to adjust your priorities and your schedule to balance your home life with your job and your education. Try to avoid overloading yourself. It's always better to take more time and to do well, than to rush things and do poorly. Remember—one step at a time. If you have children, spending time with them is no doubt a high priority in your life. Sometimes health care professionals wonder if the time they spend advancing their education and careers might have a negative impact on their children. Yet these same professionals report the benefits of setting a good example for their children—demonstrating self-discipline by studying, preparing for tests, and completing homework assignments when they would really rather be doing something else.

Don't be surprised if your goals change over time—most people's do. Don't become discouraged if attaining a goal takes much longer than you had anticipated. Adjustments and delays are just typical parts of the process as you learn more about yourself, what you want out of your career, and what's going to work best for you and your family. The important thing is that you have a plan and you're on the road to where you want to be eventually.

When the going gets rough, avoid giving up. Talk with your role model, mentor, family members, or friends for encouragement and support. You'll probably hear that just about everyone else also thought about giving up at one time or another. If your goals are worth achieving, they're worth fighting for. Hang in there.

Expect to take some risks along the way. Risk taking *does not* mean being foolish or haphazard in how you make decisions. But it *does* mean taking some well-thought-out, calculated steps that force you to stretch a little bit. After all, if you don't try, you'll never know if you could have been successful. If your goals are realistic, if you take things one step at a time, and if you apply yourself and do your best, then you stand a good chance of eventually arriving at where you want to be.

TAPPING INTO RESOURCES

Make sure you tap into all of the resources available to you. Do some research by using the library, Internet, career and occupational reference books, educational and career counselors at local schools, human resource consultants at work, and the like. As suggested earlier, read *It's a Jungle Out There! An Insider's Outlook on Jobs in Health Care* for the latest information on how jobs and career opportunities in health care are changing and what kinds of skills are in demand among employers. Check into sources of financial aid through schools and at work. Many health care employers will help support the education and training of their employees through scholarships, tuition reimbursement, employer-sponsored training, and flexible work schedules to help accommodate class time.

THE IMPRESSION YOU MAKE ON OTHERS

The impression that people have of you is an important factor in your opportunities for advancement. How you view yourself and the quality of your work might be quite different from other people's impressions of you. Learn all you can about the impression you make on others and look for ways to improve your image. Talk with your current supervisor and let him or her know you're interested in advancement. Ask your supervisor for feedback on your performance. What does your supervisor view as your strengths and your areas for improvement? How does he or she describe your interpersonal, organizational, communication, and problem-solving skills? What advice might your supervisor offer to help you grow and advance? Although you may hear some negatives, view your supervisor's feedback as **constructive criticism,** geared to make you an even better professional. When it comes time to apply for a promotion, for a different job, or for admission into an educational program, a positive recommendation from your current supervisor could be extremely important.

Networking with a variety of people can help you strengthen your interpersonal skills and learn more about job opportunities, both within your own organization and externally in other organizations throughout your community. Join a professional association or study group and consider volunteering for special projects and committees to hone your current skills, develop some new ones, and meet other people who might be able to help you grow and advance.

EXPECTING THE UNEXPECTED

The previous chapter discussed the importance of adapting to change and letting change open new doors for you. Even if you've established some goals for advancement and are well on your way to achieving them, continue to keep your eyes open for other opportunities that might arise when you least expect it. As mentioned earlier, today's health care system is in the midst of rapid change. Jobs are being redesigned, departments are being reorganized, and health care services are moving from the hospital setting to outpatient facilities. Increasing numbers of workers are being trained, cross-trained, and retrained for new responsibilities. So even if your own career goals don't include getting some additional training, your employer might expect it as part of your current job. If this type of opportunity comes your way, welcome it! Having your job redesigned will bring some major changes your way, but try to view this as a good opportunity and make it work for you. After all, health care professionals must be lifelong learners, always acquiring something new to benefit both them and the patients they serve.

RÉSUMÉS

If your goals include applying for a new job or for admission into an educational program, preparing a résumé will likely be a part of the process. Even if you don't have much postsecondary education or occupational work experience, it's still best to have a résumé. Résumés give employers and admissions committees a snapshot of your background and the qualifications you're presenting for consideration. If you've never developed a résumé, find a book at your local library or bookstore to review, or ask someone who writes or reviews resumes to help you.

Your résumé should be typed, professional in appearance, concise, and able to be scanned quickly. Avoid fancy, colored paper with borders or graphic designs.

Organize the information and make sure your grammar and spelling are correct. Emphasize your educational background and your current skills and abilities that demonstrate your qualifications for the program or job for which you are applying. Include your computer skills, even if they are only very basic, any special training sessions you've attended, certificates of completion you've earned, and letters of commendation or other types of recognition or awards you've received. Also include two or three personal and professional references who have agreed to provide additional information about you upon request. Be sure you contact these individuals before listing them on your résumé. Ask for permission to use them as references. Let them know what you're applying for and when to expect a phone call or form to fill out and return. When identifying references, select people who are familiar with the quality of your work and who have positive, insightful things to say about you. The more credible the reference, the better. Do not use relatives, for example. Also, if you already know someone who works for the training program or place of employment where you're applying, and if that person is truly familiar with you and the quality of your work, it's acceptable to list that person as a reference. But avoid "name dropping," "pulling strings," or "using connections" to try to enhance your chances of being selected. Such actions may have a negative impact on interviewers and selection committee members. Take the professional approach—stand on your own merits and get selected for the right reasons.

Submitting supportive documents with your résumé (such as letters from patients, physicians, or charge nurses thanking you or describing efforts beyond the call of duty) is usually permissible but don't get carried away. Select one or two of the best and save the others to bring along with you to the interview just in case you need them later.

APPLICATION FORMS

Whether you're applying for a new job or for admission into an educational program, it's almost certain you'll have an application form to fill out and submit. As with the résumé, the application form can be very important in the selection process. If there's a deadline, make sure your application gets submitted to the right place on time. Employers and admissions committee members review applications closely to determine if the applicant can read and follow directions. The application is also a sample of your written communication skills, so spend an adequate amount of time preparing the application form. Fill it out yourself, don't have someone else do it for you. If you type, it's best to type in the information. If you don't type, make sure your writing is legible.

Read the directions on the form carefully and then follow them. Make sure all words are spelled correctly and list accurate dates for previous work experience and education. Review the form to make sure you haven't left anything out. Stand on your own merits—don't ever falsify or exaggerate any information. Misrepresentation is dishonest and constitutes fraud. It's unprofessional, unethical, and likely to result in your dismissal should your lies ever be discovered.

If the application calls for a brief statement about why you're applying for the job or for the program, take some time to think about your answer before writing it. You'd be surprised how much weight your answer might carry in the selection process. Often, employers and program admissions committees screen applicants first to decide which applicants will get interviews and which ones won't. This screening usually involves an evaluation of the application form as well as a review of the applicant's résumé. So make sure your answer to the "why" question is well-thought-out and expressed effectively. Use your best written communication skills to convince the reviewers that you've thought about the job or the program and you know it's a good match for you, your interests, and your skills.

PREEMPLOYMENT/PREADMISSION TESTING AND RECORD REVIEWS

Don't be surprised if you're asked to take some written or practical exams to assess your current skills. Employers and admissions committee members need to know if you're qualified for the job or the program and if you have the knowledge and skills necessary to be successful. Some employers and schools schedule half-day or full-day tests and assessments to evaluate your reading, language, and math skills; work ethics and personal values; and specific skills required for certain jobs, such as a typing test. Preemployment and preadmission tests are difficult to prepare for because they measure the accumulation of the knowledge, skills, and abilities you've developed over the course of your life. So try not to be intimidated by these kinds of tests. Get plenty of sleep the night before so you're well rested, eat breakfast, and just concentrate on doing your best. If possible, ask for some feedback on how you performed on the assessments so you'll be aware of your strong and weak points. If scores indicate some weaknesses, work on strengthening these areas.

Most jobs and educational programs require either a high school diploma or a GED (General Equivalency Diploma). Depending on the job you're applying for, employers may need proof of your high school graduation or your GED. Most educational programs require both high school and college transcripts, if applicable. Many require **official transcripts,** which means the school you attended has printed the document, sealed it in an envelope, and mailed it directly to the employer or educational program without being handled by the applicant. This process prevents the applicant from tampering with the transcript prior to review by the employer or admissions committee.

If it's been several years since you graduated from high school, employers and admissions committee members may not rely on your grades to indicate your current knowledge and abilities. But if you're a recent high school graduate, your grades could be important. On the other hand, grades from college courses are often important, especially when applying for admission into an educational program. If the courses you took directly apply to the job or the educational program you're seeking, and if you got good grades, your college transcript can be of great value in the selection process. Even if the courses you took do not apply directly to the job or program you're seeking, the fact that you've proven your ability to handle college-level course work is a plus.

Employers and admissions committee members are usually impressed by applicants who can manage a job, school, and a personal life at the same time. On the other hand, they're often concerned about applicants with attendance problems. If you've had a poor attendance record in the past, this could pose a problem during the selection process, especially if you're applying for a new job. If the new job you're applying for is in the company where you currently work, your attendance and performance records for your current job and all previous jobs are usually made available to the people making selection decisions for the new job. So, if you're on an attendance warning or some other form of corrective action in your current position, you might have to clean up your record first before being considered for another position.

PREPARING FOR AN INTERVIEW

Once you've submitted your application form, résumé, and any supporting documents and made it past the first screening, you're ready to prepare for the personal interview. Making a good impression during an interview pulls together just about everything we've discussed in this book. Your objective is to present yourself as a qualified, motivated health care professional who is well prepared for the new job or for admission into an educational program. Don't just show up for an interview. Do your homework first.

Learn as much as you can about the job and the employer, or the school and the program, ahead of time so you can talk intelligently about the opportunity for which you are applying. For example, if you're applying for a job in an outpatient clinic, find out what kinds of patients are seen there, what services are provided on site, what kinds of workers are employed there, what hours the clinic is open, and so on. If you're applying for admission into an educational program, find out about the history of the program and the school, what types of students enroll, who makes up the faculty, what other programs are offered, what degrees or certificates are awarded, what agencies accredit the program, and the like. If you appear for an interview and aren't familiar with basic information about the company or the school, interviewers might wonder if you're really serious about being selected or not. If you take the time to investigate the company or school first, interviewers are more likely to be impressed with your interest and may give you some extra consideration.

Even if you've already been asked why you're applying for the job or the educational program on the application form, you'll probably be asked that same question again during the interview. Knowing as much as you can about the job or program you're applying for will help convince interviewers that you've given this question a lot of thought and that you're sure you're a good match for the opening. Someone may ask what you did to investigate the job or the profession you would be training for. Having done research at the library and on the Internet, job shadowing, and talking with people who know what's involved, you'll have several examples to share with interviewers.

Think about the kinds of questions you might be asked during the interview and decide how you would answer each one. Practice at home with someone firing questions at you in a mock interview setting. Why are you interested in this job or program? What have you done to investigate it? How much do you know about it? How can you be sure it's right for you? What do you think it would take to be successful in this job or program? What have you done to prepare yourself for the job or program? What difficulties would you foresee? What strengths would you bring to the job or the program? What are your weaknesses and what are you doing to overcome them? What's an example of a difficult challenge that you've faced and managed to overcome? Why should we accept you over other candidates? What will you do if you're not accepted for this job or this program? The more questions you can anticipate in advance, the better prepared you will be.

Get plenty of sleep the night before your interview and eat a good breakfast or lunch before your appointment. Make sure you arrive on time and at the right location. If you aren't absolutely sure you know where you're going and how to get there, allow plenty of extra time to avoid being late. If for some reason you are unable to be there at the appointed time, call and let the appropriate person know. Remember, you get only one chance to make a good first impression. Also allow plenty of time for the interview itself. Other applicants may be scheduled for interviews during the same time period as you, so interviewers could be running late and you might be kept waiting.

PARTICIPATING IN AN INTERVIEW

Once you've prepared for the interview and appeared at the right time and place, it's important to make a positive, professional impression. Start by looking your very best. If you wear a uniform in your current job and your interview takes place just before, after, or during your regular work hours, either take a change of clothing to wear for the interview, or make absolutely certain your uniform is impeccably clean and pressed. Avoid clothing, hairstyles, or items that might distract interviewers or elicit an undesirable reaction. Examples include miniskirts, hair that glows in the dark, and nose rings. Remember, you want interviewers to remember you based on your qualifications, not your outlandish attire. Good grooming is essential, including clean hair, clean fingernails, and polished shoes. Think twice about long, brightly colored fingernails; they aren't acceptable in many types of health care jobs. Keep jewelry and other accessories to a minimum.

Smile, offer a firm handshake, and try to remember the names of the people who are introduced to you. Apply your best interpersonal communication skills. It's OK to be nervous—in fact interviewers might wonder what's wrong with you if you aren't nervous! But maintain your composure and be confident and self-assured. Let interviewers know what skills and abilities you would bring to the job or to the educational program, and how you would be an asset and a good team player for the organization. Don't just fabricate a bunch of words that might sound insincere. If you've done an adequate job of preparing for your interview, you've already identified some good examples of personal and professional traits that you can share with interviewers.

Sit up straight, don't chew gum or bite your fingernails, and try to relax! Don't be surprised if you're interviewed by more than one person, perhaps at the same time. Having one person fire questions at you can be intimidating enough without having two or three people doing the same thing during the same session. Sometimes employers and admissions committees have no choice but to have multiple people interview a candidate at the same time. In some cases, it's done intentionally to see how well a candidate performs under pressure.

Concentrate on each question and think before you answer. You may be given a "what if?" question to test your thinking skills. What would you do if . . . ? Don't just blurt out the first thought that pops into your mind. But don't ponder the question too long either. Interviewers need to know if you can analyze situations and think quickly. Put your best critical-thinking and problem-solving skills to work and answer these kinds of questions to the best of your ability.

In order to prevent discrimination in the selection process, there are several questions that interviewers are supposed to avoid asking. These questions relate to personal characteristics such as your age, sexual lifestyle preferences (heterosexual, homosexual, bisexual), marital status, and plans for becoming pregnant. Unfortunately, some interviewers do ask inappropriate questions, so it's important to anticipate these questions in advance and be prepared to respond.

The interviewing process is not a one-way street—it's OK for you to ask questions, too. In fact, many interviewers give candidates extra points for asking good questions. Write your questions in advance and take them with you to the interview. When your questions are answered, jot down the responses along with any other information you don't want to forget. Interviewers will notice that you pay attention to details and recognize the need to record important information. Avoid asking questions that are already answered in whatever printed materials may have been made available to you in advance. If you ask a question that's already been discussed in a brochure, for example, the interviewer may wonder if you even read the material.

Not everyone agrees on whether or not to ask questions about pay and benefits during the first interview for a new job. Although most would agree that pay and benefits are important, it's usually best to discuss the primary responsibilities of the job and the type of candidate the company is looking for first. If you know there's going to be a follow-up interview, wait for that appointment to ask about pay and benefits. Or, let the interviewer take the lead in bringing up the discussion. Do give some thought ahead of time to what your pay and benefit requirements would be in case you are asked that question during your interview. Don't respond "I don't know" or "I haven't really thought about it." These answers indicate you haven't done your homework. Before the interview, talk with someone in human resources or a manager in the area where you would be working to find out the pay range for the position for which you've applied. Think about the pay you're making in your current job and how much more, if any, you would expect to be paid in the new job. It's OK to say "It's negotiable" but have an acceptable range in mind.

When applying for admission into an educational program, ask if the program is accredited. **Educational accreditation** means the program has met the standards set forth by professional associations or other organizations concerned with quality outcomes. Accreditation is *not* required for all types of educational programs, but *graduating from an accredited program* may be a requirement for a license, professional certification, or some other type of credential. When investigating educational programs, be sure you're aware of all expenses to attend, including tuition, books, uniforms, and supplies. Also be sure you know the average starting pay for program graduates and where the best employment opportunities can be found. Ask interviewers how many students are accepted into the program and how many usually complete it successfully. What percent of students find jobs in the local area right after graduation? What percent of graduates pass national certification exams on the first attempt?

In many situations, it's a nice idea to write a short note thanking the employer or the school for considering your application and granting you an interview. Doing so demonstrates courtesy and good manners, and it also puts your name in front of the decision makers one more time.

In summary, pull together everything you've learned about professionalism and apply it to the application, interviewing, and selection process. If you get selected, you'll be on the road to achieving another goal. If you don't get accepted, you'll know you did your best and you will have learned something in the process. If you feel you are truly qualified, don't give up. Employers and admissions committee members value perseverance. Ask for feedback on how to enhance your qualifications. Then follow the advice and reapply a second time. It's not unusual for candidates to be turned down the first time and then accepted on the second attempt. If you reapply and are turned down a second time, it's probably wise to work with an adviser to help you decide if your goal needs to be revised somewhat.

IN SUMMARY

Each day presents an opportunity to learn something new. Continually rethink your goals, make sure you're on the path to success, and keep getting better and better. If you can live up to your own expectations and know, in your heart, that you're a health care professional, you're well on your way to a productive and rewarding career.

Good luck with your journey—and enjoy each and every step along the way.

GLOSSARY OF TERMS

stagnant   without motion, dull, sluggish

potential   an ability that can, but has not yet, come into being

dynamic   in motion, energetic and vigorous

occupational preferences   the types of work and work settings than an individual prefers

job shadowing   observing workers to see what their jobs are like

transferable skills   skills acquired in one job that are applicable in another job

multiskilled   cross-trained to provide more than one function, often in more than one discipline

personal assessments   questionnaires and tests that identify interests and evaluate abilities

basic skills   fundamental aptitudes in reading, language, and math

goal   an object or end that one strives to attain; an aim

role model   a person that another person aspires to be like

mentor   a wise, loyal adviser

postsecondary   after high school

constructive criticism   viewing one's weaknesses in a way that leads to positive improvement

networking   interacting with a variety of people in different settings

official transcripts   grade reports that are printed, sealed, and mailed directly to the recipient to prevent tampering by the applicant

educational accreditation   acknowledgment that an educational program has met the quality outcome standards of a professional association or other organization

✎ EXERCISES

Complete the following.

1) Think about the history of your career, where it stands now, and where it's headed. Is your career stagnant or dynamic?

_____

_____

_____

_____

_____

_____

2) Describe the "dream" you have for your career, ways you can develop your potential, and plans for enjoying your journey along the way.

_____

_____

_____

_____

_____

_____

3) Describe:
   a) your occupational preferences (the kind of work and work setting you prefer)

_____

_____

_____

_____

_____

_____

   b) your abilities (your current knowledge and skills)

_____

_____

_____

_____

_____

_____

   c) your aptitude (your ability to learn more)

_____

_____

_____

_____

_____

4) Have you ever taken personal assessments? If so, describe what you learned from them.

_____

_____

_____

_____

_____

_____

_____

5) Describe your basic skills. Are they sufficiently strong to support further growth and development? Why or why not?

_____

_____

_____

_____

_____

_____

6) List some employment opportunities where you live that might be of interest to you, and explain where and how you learned about these opportunities.

_____

_____

_____

_____

_____

7) Identify your "transferable skills" and explain which of these skills could be applied in jobs and in employment settings of interest to you.

_____

_____

_____

_____

_____

8) Have you set goals for your career? If yes, list your short-term and long-term goals. If no, what needs to occur before setting your goals?

_____

_____

_____

_____

_____

_____

9) Describe someone who's been a role model in your life. How did having a role model help you?

_____

_____

_____

_____

_____

_____

10) Describe someone who's been a mentor for you. How did your mentor help you?

_____

_____

_____

_____

_____

_____

11) Have you been a role model or mentor for someone else? If so, describe the experience and what it meant to you and to the other person.

_____

_____

_____

_____

_____

_____

12) Think back to the last time a supervisor, teacher, or someone else gave you some constructive criticism. Did it help you? Why or why not?

_____

_____

_____

_____

_____

_____

_____

13) If you have applied for a new job or for admission into an educational program and did not get selected, how did not being selected make you feel? What did you do as a result? Looking back on the situation, if you had it to do over again, what, if anything, would you do differently?

_____

_____

_____

_____

_____

_____

_____

SELF-ASSESSMENT

Think about yourself and how you approach your work. Consider each of the following and check all that apply.

_____ 1) I recognize the importance of having a dynamic career and developing my potential.

_____ 2) I think about my career and have a plan for where it's headed.

_____ 3) I plan for tomorrow but I live for today.

_____ 4) I'm aware of my transferable skills and how they could apply in other jobs and in other employment settings.

_____ 5) I've taken advantage of personal assessments and am familiar with my occupational interests, abilities, and aptitude for learning more.

_____ 6) I'm aware of employment opportunities in the area where I live.

_____ 7) My basic skills are sufficiently strong to support advanced learning.

_____ 8) I recognize the value of job shadowing when exploring career choices.

_____ 9) I plan ahead, take things one step at a time, and avoid rushing into situations for which I might not be prepared.

_____ 10) I have set both short-term and long-term goals for my career.

_____ 11) I am comfortable with the fact that my goals may change over time.

_____ 12) I have benefited from having a role model or mentor.

_____ 13) I recognize the importance of being a role model or a mentor for other people.

_____ **14)** I network with other people to strengthen my interpersonal skills and learn more about job opportunities.

_____ **15)** I know that career advancement involves taking some well-thought-out, calculated risks.

_____ **16)** I'm aware of career resources available to me and I take advantage of them.

_____ **17)** I view constructive criticism as valuable feedback that can help me improve even more.

_____ **18)** My résumé is professional in appearance and accurately reflects my background and qualifications.

_____ **19)** I make sure application forms are complete, accurate, and submitted on time.

_____ **20)** I would never falsify information on an application form or on a résumé.

_____ **21)** I prepare in advance for interviews.

_____ **22)** I make a positive and professional impression during interviews.

_____ **23)** When not selected for a job or an educational program, I make sure my goal is realistic, ask for feedback on how to improve my qualifications, and reapply at a later date.

✐ INDIVIDUAL NEXT-STEP ACTION PLANS

Based on your Self-Assessment, complete the following.

1) My strongest skills are:

_____

_____

_____

_____

_____

_____

_____

2) My areas for improvement are:

_____

_____

_____

_____

_____

_____

3) Five things I plan to do to improve my skills:

    a) _____

    b) _____

c) _____

d) _____

e) _____

✍ WHAT IF SCENARIOS

What would you do in the following situations?

1) You've been in the same job for three years, and you're starting to get bored with the routine. You're wondering if it might be time to try something else.

_____

_____

_____

_____

_____

_____

_____

2) You've noticed workers in another department who appear to have a more interesting job than your own.

_____

_____

_____

_____

_____

_____

_____

3) You've moved to a new town and need to find a good job.

_____

_____

_____

_____

_____

_____

_____

4) You work in a hospital but are thinking about applying for a job in an outpatient clinic owned by the same health network. You're wondering if the training and work experience you've had in the past would make you qualified for this new position.

_____

_____

_____

_____

_____

_____

_____

5) You'd like to obtain a B.S. degree at a local college, but you've never taken a college course before.

_____

_____

_____

_____

_____

_____

_____

6) The new job you're thinking about applying for requires math skills, but you don't know if your math is strong enough to do the job well.

_____

_____

_____

_____

_____

_____

_____

7) You're happy in your current job but would like to acquire some new skills to keep you challenged.

_____

_____

_____

_____

_____

_____

8) You're meeting with your supervisor or your educational program director for your regularly scheduled performance feedback session.

_____

_____

_____

_____

_____

_____

9) You're planning to apply for a new job or for admission into an educational program. Your résumé is two years old and you aren't sure how effective it might be.

_____

_____

_____

_____

_____

_____

10) You've been asked to complete an application form for a new job or for admission into an educational program. The deadline for submitting applications is tomorrow morning and you're pressed for time.

_____

_____

_____

_____

_____

_____

_____

11) The job you're interested in requires three years of previous work experience. You have only two and one-half years of work experience but could easily adjust the dates to indicate a full three years.

_____

_____

_____

_____

_____

_____

12) The educational program you're applying for requires a grade-point average of 3.0 on a 4.0 scale. Due to poor performance last semester, your grade-point average is only a 2.0. Because the admissions committee did not require an official transcript, it would be easy to white out the 2.0 on your transcript and change it to a 3.0. After all, once you're in the program, you know you can pass the courses.

_____

_____

_____

_____

_____
_____
_____

13) After deciding to apply for a new job in an outpatient clinic, you find out your mother knows the clinic's human resource manager. Just a few months ago, your mother helped him refinance his home mortgage, and your mother has offered to make a phone call to the HR manager on your behalf.

_____
_____
_____
_____
_____
_____
_____

14) On the morning of your interview, your car won't start and you have no other means of transportation.

_____
_____
_____
_____
_____
_____

15) The only interview appointment that's open is at 4 P.M. on Wednesday. You're scheduled to work at your current job up until 3:30 P.M. that day. Your supervisor has told you and your coworkers to wear blue jeans or other old clothes that day because you'll be moving supplies and setting up a new inventory room.

_____
_____
_____
_____
_____
_____

16) During your interview, you are asked the following questions:
- Why have you applied for this job (or educational program)?
- What are your strengths?
- What is your biggest weakness?
- What do you dislike about your current job?

- If you could, what would you change about your current supervisor?
- Why should we select you?
- What will you do if you don't get selected?

_____

_____

_____

_____

_____

_____

_____

17) After applying for your "dream" job or for admission into an educational program that represents a major goal in your career, you don't get selected.

_____

_____

_____

_____

_____

_____

_____

_____

✍ REVIEW QUESTIONS

Answer each of the following.

1) Describe the difference between a stagnant career and a dynamic career.

_____

_____

_____

_____

_____

_____

_____

2) What are occupational preferences?

_____

_____

_____

_____

_____

_____

_____

3) What is job shadowing and how can it help in career exploration?

_____

_____

_____

_____

_____

_____

4) What are transferable skills and how do they apply in career planning?

_____

_____

_____

_____

_____

_____

5) What are abilities and aptitude?

_____

_____

_____

_____

_____

_____

6) What are personal assessments and why are they important?

_____

_____

_____

_____

_____

_____

7) What are basic skills and why are they important?

_____

_____

_____

_____

_____

8) Define *goals,* *short-term goals,* and *long-term goals,* and explain why goals are important.

_____

_____

_____

_____

_____

_____

_____

9) Describe what is meant by setting "realistic" goals, and explain how a role model and mentor can help you make sure your goals are attainable.

_____

_____

_____

_____

_____

_____

_____

10) Why should you be a role model and mentor for other people?

_____

_____

_____

_____

_____

_____

_____

11) What is postsecondary education?

_____

_____

_____

_____

_____

_____

_____

12) Why is it a good idea to take just one college course first?

_____

_____

_____

_____

_____

_____

_____

13) What role does risk taking play in career advancement?

_____

_____

_____

_____

_____

_____

14) List three resources that can help you with career advancement.

_____

_____

_____

_____

_____

_____

15) What is constructive criticism and how can it help you?

_____

_____

_____

_____

_____

_____

_____

16) What is networking and why is it valuable?

_____

_____

_____

_____

_____

_____

17) Discuss the importance of "expecting the unexpected."

_____

_____

_____

_____

_____

_____

_____

18) What is a résumé?

_____

_____

_____

_____

_____

_____

_____

19) Why is an application form an important part of the selection process?

_____

_____

_____

_____

_____

_____

_____

20) List three important factors in completing and submitting an application form appropriately.

_____

_____

_____

_____

_____

_____

_____

21) What is preemployment or preadmission testing and why is it done?

_____

_____

_____

_____

_____

_____

_____

22) What are official transcripts?

_____

_____

_____

_____

_____
_____
_____

23) List five important factors in participating in an interview for a new job or for admission into a training program.

_____
_____
_____
_____
_____
_____
_____

24) Explain why it's important never to falsify or exaggerate information about yourself on an application form or during an interview.

_____
_____
_____
_____
_____
_____

25) Why is it important to pull together everything you've learned about professionalism during the application, interviewing, and selection process?

_____
_____
_____
_____
_____
_____
_____

(Answers to Review Questions are at the end of the book.)

Answers to Review Questions

CHAPTER ONE: MAKING A COMMITMENT TO YOUR JOB

1. Describe a health care "professional."

Professionals have a way of "being," "knowing," and "doing" that sets them apart from others. Professionalism brings together who you are as a person, what you value, how you treat other people, what you contribute in the workplace, and how seriously you take your job. Professionals are good at what they do and like doing it. They enjoy helping others and knowing they've made a difference. They have their personal "act" together and it shows. They set high standards for performance and achieve them. They see the "big picture" in health care and know where they fit in. They care about quality and how to improve it. They treat everyone they meet with dignity and respect. They continually strive to grow and learn.

2. What does it mean to take a professional approach to one's job?

Taking a professional approach to one's job means applying the concepts of professionalism every day. It means knowing that other people are counting on you to be there, to be on time, to be reliable, and to follow through. It means having a strong work ethic, being accountable and competent, complying with laws and policies, and representing your employer's mission and values in a positive way.

3. List ten jobs that require professionalism.

Any ten health care jobs because *all* health care jobs require professionalism.

4. Why is it important to be aware of trends in health care?

People who don't work in health care look to people who do for information or advice. Health care professionals must be aware of what's going on in their industry and be able to talk intelligently about it with other people.

5. Discuss what is meant by a systems perspective.

A systems perspective means stepping back to view an entire process to see how each component connects with the others.

6. Define *corrective action.*

Corrective action is when steps are taken to overcome a job performance problem.

7. List five actions that could result in your getting dismissed from your job.

You could get dismissed from your job for poor attendance, poor punctuality, insubordination, failure to perform your job in a competent manner, failure to comply with laws or policies, breaching confidentiality, sexually harassing someone, creating a hostile workplace, being involved in a conflict of interest, fraudulent billing, up-coding insurance forms, improperly changing or destroying records, theft, accepting pay for hours not worked, working outside your scope of practice, failing to maintain required credentials, and other unethical or illegal acts.

8. What is competence?

Possessing the necessary knowledge and skills to perform your job appropriately and safely on a daily basis.

9. Define *reliable, accountable,* and *diligent.* Give one example of each.

Reliable means you're trustworthy and can be counted upon; an example would be following through when you've told someone you can be counted on to do something. Accountable means you accept responsibility and the consequences of your actions; an example would be admitting when you've made a mistake rather than blaming someone else. Diligent means being careful in your work; an example would be paying attention to details so that something doesn't "fall through the cracks."

10. What does it mean to make a commitment to your job? Give one example of being committed and one example of not being committed.

Making a commitment to your job means taking it seriously, applying yourself, and doing your best. It requires pulling together all of the knowledge, skills, compassion, and commitment needed to make you the very best employee you can possibly be. An example of a committed worker would be one who pays attention to detail and is careful. A worker who is not committed to his or her work would not pay attention to detail and be sloppy. Other examples of commitment or a lack of commitment could relate to work ethic, attendance and punctuality, competency, compliance, and confidentiality.

11. What is a strong "work ethic" and why is it important to employers?
A strong work ethic means applying attitudes and behaviors that support good work performance. It means positioning your job as a high priority in your life and making sound decisions about how you approach your work. It's important for employers to have employees with a strong work ethic so that the organization can get its work done and meet its customers' needs in a professional and efficient manner.

12. What should you do if you make a mistake?
Admit your mistake and accept full responsibility. Remedy the situation, apologize to anyone who's been inconvenienced, learn from the experience, and avoid making the same mistake twice.

13. Why are good attendance and punctuality so important?
Other people are counting on you to perform the duties of your job, so you must show up for work every day and be on time.

14. What's a contingency plan? Give an example.
A contingency plan is a backup plan in case the original plan doesn't work. Examples include having alternative transportation in case your car breaks down or the bus is late, or making alternative child-care arrangements in case your child or your spouse gets sick.

15. Define *insubordination* and give an example.
Insubordination is the refusal to complete an assigned task. Examples would include refusing to accept a work assignment or to participate in certain types of patient care procedures.

16. What is corporate compliance, and why is it becoming even more important today than it has been in the past?
Corporate compliance means acting in accordance with laws and with a company's rules, policies, and procedures. It's gaining even more attention today because the government is stepping up its efforts to identify violators and prosecute them.

17. List three examples of compliance issues.

Examples of compliance issues include confidentiality, safety and environmental precautions, labor laws, retention of records, Medicare billing and reimbursement, licensing and credentials, conflict of interest, illegal and unethical behaviors, sexual harassment, and theft and other dishonest acts.

18. What is a whistle blower?

A whistle blower is someone who exposes the illegal or unethical practices of another person or of a company.

19. What is confidentiality and why is it important?

Confidentiality is maintaining the privacy of certain matters. It's both legally and ethically imperative to protect the confidentiality of patient records, financial reports, and other materials your employer deems private. Failure to do so could result in dismissal from your job.

20. What is sexual harassment?

Sexual harassment is making unwelcome, sexually oriented advances or comments to another person.

21. What is a hostile workplace?

A hostile workplace is an uncomfortable or unsafe work environment.

22. What is a scope of practice and why is it important?

A scope of practice is the boundaries that determine what a worker may and may not do as part of his or her job. Performing duties beyond what you're legally permitted to do is highly risky, may be illegal, and could result in dismissal from your job.

23. What is the difference between a license and a certification?

Licenses, granted by state agencies, award legal permission to practice. Other people, without such a license, are legally barred from practicing. Certification, awarded by a state agency or a professional association, awards permission to use a special professional title. Other people, without such a certification, may legally practice but are not permitted to use the special professional title.

24. Define *conflict of interest* and give an example.

Conflict of interest is an inappropriate relationship between personal interests and official responsibilities. An example would be awarding a contract to an outside company and then accepting a personal gift or free meals in exchange for doing so. Other examples include asking one of your company's vendors for a discount on a personal purchase, or referring patients to one of your relatives.

25. Discuss what is meant by "*You* are the company you work for."

Even though you don't own the business you work for, it's still "your" company. You should take pride in the company you work for, keep up on the latest events, support your employer, and have a sense of ownership.

26. What are corporate mission and corporate values? Why is it important for employees to support the mission and values of the company they work for?

A corporate mission is the special duties, functions, or purposes of a company. Corporate values are those beliefs held in high esteem by a company. It's important to support your company's mission and values because you are a representative of that company. To patients, visitors, guests, and vendors, you *are* the company.

27. Define *discretion* and explain why it's important.

Discretion means being careful about what one says and does. Regardless of what job you have, your appearance, attitudes, and behaviors reflect the company you work for. It's important to be careful what you say and do because your actions can affect the reputation of the company.

28. What is a vendor?

Vendors are people who work for companies with which your company does business.

29. What are front-line workers and how do they influence a company's reputation?

Front-line workers are employees who have the most frequent contact with a company's customers. Their appearance, attitudes, and behaviors reflect the company they work for and influence the reputation of that company.

CHAPTER TWO: PERSONAL TRAITS OF THE HEALTH CARE PROFESSIONAL

1. Discuss what is meant by "Professionalism brings together who you are as a person and how you contribute those traits in the workplace."

Before you can achieve success "doing" something, you have to "be" something. Being a health care professional depends greatly on who you are as a person. Your character and values give direction to your behavior, and ultimately result in your reputation as a professional.

2. Explain why employers are putting more emphasis on the character of their employees.

A lack of character among employees is causing major problems for employers. These include employee theft, sleeping or watching television on the job, engaging in sexual activities with coworkers on the job, falsifying information, filing fraudulent claims, engaging in arguments and fights, and sometimes even committing "angel of mercy" murders.

3. Define *character* and list five character traits.
Character is a person's moral behavior and qualities. Character traits include honesty, morals, integrity, trustworthiness, ethics, and respect.

4. List five workplace problems that can be traced back to a lack of character among employees.
These include theft, absenteeism, dishonesty, workplace violence, substance abuse, safety infractions, negligence, and low productivity.

5. Define *reputation* and list five factors that influence it.
Reputation is a person's character, values, and behavior as viewed by others. Factors that influence a person's reputation include honesty, knowing the difference between right and wrong, sound judgment, self-control, positive relationships with others, sharing, fairness, respect, ethics, loyalty, and a sense of priorities.

6. What is judgment?
Judgment is comparison of options to decide which is best. Judgment helps us make the best decisions-such as what to do, why to do it, how to do it, when to do it, where to do it, and whom to do it with.

7. What is a conscience and what role does it play in making decisions?
A conscience is moral judgment that prohibits or opposes the violation of a previously recognized ethical principle. It's the little voice that gnaws away at you, keeps you from sleeping at night, and constantly says, "You *know* this *isn't* the right thing to do!" Your conscience reminds you of the difference between right and wrong and helps you make ethical decisions.

8. List three questions to ask yourself when making a difficult decision.
Ask: What are my choices? How do the options compare with one another? What might happen? Who might be affected? How would it make me feel? How would my decision be viewed by other people? What would my supervisor think? How would my coworkers feel? Could I lose my job? Other questions include: How would this look if it appeared in the newspapers? How would my children feel? Would my family support me? Could I look myself in the mirror? Would I be able to sleep at night?

9. Explain why it's difficult to build trust but easy to lose it.

In today's society, we've become increasingly suspicious of other people. "Don't trust anyone!" is common advice. It takes a long time for people to learn to trust you, and only one quick incident to lose someone's trust.

10. Explain what is meant by "A professional's word is good as gold."

This means that people can count on you and know they can trust you to be there when you're supposed to be, to perform the responsibilities of your job with competence, and to keep your promises and meet your obligations.

11. Give two examples of cheating.

Cheating includes referring to your notes during a closed-book test, using someone else's information and claiming it's your own, keeping things that don't belong to you, and calling in sick when you really aren't.

12. Explain why a "little white lie" doesn't remain "little" for long.

"Little white lies" usually snowball into big, complicated lies that can become difficult to manage. Lies are eventually uncovered, and before long, people will wonder if they can believe *anything* you say.

13. Define *fraud* and give two examples.

Fraud is intentional deceit through false information or misrepresentation. Fraud is not only dishonest, it's illegal. Examples include misrepresenting your education, credentials, or work experience on a job application, résumé, or other document; billing an insurance company for a patient procedure that never occurred; back-dating a legal document; entering incorrect data on equipment maintenance records; and changing results of a research study.

14. Give two examples of how morals and ethics can affect someone's reputation.

The capability of differentiating between right and wrong (morals) and to practice high standards of conduct and moral judgment (ethics) affect a person's reputation because they both play a major role in decision making and behavior. Every decision you make and every action you take can either build or erode someone's trust in you. One unethical decision can destroy your reputation, and one illegal act can cause you to be fired from your job—or worse.

15. List three things you can do to earn people's respect.

You can earn people's respect by being honest, trustworthy, reliable, and ethical.

Chapter Three: Working with Others

1. Discuss interdependence among health care workers and explain why it's important.

Health care workers must rely on one another to get the work done. No one person can do it all; only groups of people working together can get the job done and done well.

2. List five factors that support strong interpersonal relationships among coworkers.

Factors that support strong interpersonal relationships among coworkers include trust, honesty, ethics, fairness, treating coworkers like customers, positive attitude, optimistic outlook, inclusion, and supporting the growth and development of others.

3. List five ways you can get to know your coworkers better to improve teamwork and interpersonal relationships.

Get to know your coworkers better and let them get to know you. Invite people to join you for lunch. Be inclusive and avoid participating in cliques. Volunteer to serve on committees and sign up for employer-sponsored classes and recreational activities. Share information, space, equipment, and supplies. Laugh at yourself and be a good sport. Avoid arrogance and don't be a snob. Never "look down" on other people or treat them in a demeaning way. Treat others as you would want to be treated yourself. Acknowledge the accomplishments of others and give them credit for their efforts. Be cooperative, patient, and forgiving.

4. Why are coworkers viewed as customers? Give three other examples of health care customers.

Coworkers are your "internal" customers. Other customers are patients, visitors, guests, vendors, and physicians.

5. Who are colleagues?
Colleagues are fellow workers in the same profession.

6. Describe what it means to be loyal to your coworkers and to your employer. Give an example of each.

With coworkers, loyalty means being there for one another, to lend a helping hand or a shoulder to cry on when things get stressful. It means always being ready to help—providing encouragement, emotional support, and understanding. Loyalty to your employer means giving your job your best effort, expressing appreciation to management, and letting your supervisor know it makes you feel proud to be part of the company. When your employer invests in your education, you should continue working there for a reasonable length of time after training rather than resigning and taking your new skills across town to go to work for the competition.

7. What are self-esteem and self-worth? What impact do you have on someone else's self-esteem and self-worth?

Self-esteem is belief in oneself and having self-respect. Self-worth is recognizing importance and value in oneself. A person's self-esteem and self-worth result from the feedback we get from others, so each of us influences the self-esteem and self-worth of other people.

8. What are cliques? Why is it best to be inclusive?

Cliques are small, exclusive circles of people. Cliques exclude people, making them feel left out of the group. It's best to be inclusive rather than exclusive to avoid hurting people's feelings and to help strengthen their self-esteem and self-worth.

9. State "the golden rule" and describe why it's important in relationships.

The golden rule, "Do unto others as you would have them do unto you," is important in relationships because if you fail to treat people fairly and with respect, the interdependence that is so important in health care will be jeopardized. Nothing can make your job more pleasant or miserable than relationships at work.

10. What is synergy? How does it apply to relationships at work?

Synergy is energy created through cooperative action when working with other people. A group can accomplish so much more than people working independently as individuals. Relationships with colleagues can enrich your life and add a whole new dimension to friendship.

11. What is consensus? What makes it different from majority rules? Why is consensus important?

Consensus is a decision that all members agree to support. With majority rules, there are winners and there are losers—the majority wins and the minority loses. The objective of consensus is to arrive at a win-win resolution. Operating by consensus is the underpinning of good teamwork.

12. What are group norms and why are they important? Give three examples.

Group norms are standards, models, or patterns for a group—guidelines that help the group function well. Examples include every member is expected to participate in decision making, each person's opinion will be listened to and respected, all members will do their share of the work, and no one may leave until the team's work has been completed.

13. What is a multiskilled worker? Give two examples. List two benefits of employing multiskilled workers.

Multiskilled workers have been cross-trained to perform more than one function, often in more than one discipline. Examples include a housekeeper cross-trained to perform basic maintenance and repair duties, a nursing assistant learning to draw blood and prepare specimens for laboratory analysis, a unit secretary learning to admit patients and process bills, and a maintenance worker acquiring carpentry skills. Multiskilled workers tend to be highly productive. They can provide more services than individuals working independently and can enhance convenience for patients. They bring versatility and flexibility to the staffing plan, and they save the company some money in labor costs.

14. Define *diversity* and list five examples of cultural differences.

Diversity means differences, dissimilarities, and variations. Cultural differences include gender, age, race, ethnic background, lifestyle preferences, socioeconomic status, and physical condition. In health care, another cultural difference is the occupation in which you work, such as with registered nurses, physicians, pharmacists, secretaries, or environmental services personnel.

15. Why is it important to find "common ground" among health care workers?

Focusing on common ground gives diverse groups of workers something to build upon in overcoming their differences. Regardless of cultural differences, health care workers are all there for the same purpose—to provide high-quality health care and support services.

16. What are manners and why are they important in the workplace?

Manners are standards of behavior based on thoughtfulness and consideration of other people. Manners and common courtesy are just "common sense" for health care professionals as part of good customer service and in maintaining effective relationships with coworkers.

17. List five examples of good manners.

Examples of good manners include asking others before adjusting room temperature or playing music on the radio, returning borrowed items as soon as possible and in the same condition as when you borrowed them, repairing or replacing something you've borrowed and broken, not expecting other people to clean up after you, avoiding actions that might offend others, saying "please" and "thank you," listening while other people are talking, holding doors open for people, helping lost people find their way, practicing good elevator etiquette, and offering your seat to another person.

18. Explain why communication skills are the basis for effective relationships.

Communication skills are the basis for effective relationships because you must be able to communicate effectively to get along with people and to complete your work appropriately. Because you work in a stressful environment and with diverse groups of people, you cannot help but experience some difficulties getting along with everyone. Good communication skills support teamwork and conflict resolution.

19. What is conflict resolution and why is it important?

Conflict resolution means overcoming disagreements between two or more people. When you have a conflict with someone, it must get resolved or the situation will only get worse. Health care workers must have good communication skills and the ability to resolve conflicts in order to get along with people and to get the work done.

20. List four communication styles. Which one is most effective in conflict resolution and why?

The four styles of communication are aggressive, passive, passive-aggressive, and assertive. Assertive communication is the most effective in conflict resolution. In assertive communication, you state your opinion openly and honestly, but in a way that shows respect and consideration for the other person. This approach presents the best opportunity for both people to work together, to compromise, and to reach a win-win resolution.

21. What is a win-win resolution and why is it important?

A win-win resolution is the goal of conflict resolution—to find a solution that's acceptable to both parties. This type of resolution is important so that each person feels his or her issues have been heard, opinions have been respected, needs have been met, and that neither party ends up feeling like a "loser."

22. List five examples of good customer service.

Examples of good customer service include providing reassurance and confidence that patients are "in good hands," always presenting a positive and professional image, accepting and valuing differences, treating everyone with respect, protecting privacy and confidentiality, demonstrating compassion and concern, anticipating needs and being ready to meet them, using terms that people can understand, and appropriately referring any questions or requests that you cannot fulfill yourself to the appropriate person. Other examples include giving accurate directions on how to find a certain location, offering visitors refreshments, making a telephone available to someone who's been paged, being respectful of people's time and explaining why they have to wait and for how long, and in general making people feel comfortable and welcome.

Chapter Four: Personal Skills and the Health Care Professional

1. What are "personal skills" and how do they affect success as a health care worker?

Personal skills are abilities to manage aspects of your life outside of work. When you have good personal skills, your personal affairs are in order, freeing you up to concentrate on your job and your career. Personal skills transfer to the workplace and influence your reputation as a professional. This includes your personal image; your ability to manage time, finances, stress, and change; and your critical-thinking and problem-solving skills.

2. List five personal appearance and grooming traits that support an *un*professional image.

Appearance and grooming traits that support an unprofessional image include a ripped uniform, dirty shoes, oily hair, grimy fingernails, and body odor. Other examples include clothing that is too tight, too short, or too revealing. Also excessive makeup, inappropriate jewelry, strong perfume or aftershave, hair in the face, and poor posture. Nose rings, pierced body parts, neon hair, spiked haircuts, tattoos, and extra-long fingernails are also examples.

3. Describe how a health care worker's personal image affects the patients he or she serves.

One of the first things people notice about you is the image you portray. Patients need to have confidence in their caregivers, and family members and friends who visit patients need reassurance that their loved ones are being cared for by professionals. Unprofessional appearance reflects badly on the company and might leave patients, family members, and friends wondering if a person's unprofessional appearance might also indicate a lack of competence in his or her work.

4. What is a dress code and why is it important?

A dress code is a company's standards for attire and appearance. The personal appearance of workers reflects directly upon the reputation of the company.

5. List three examples of personal habits that support an *un*professional image.

Examples include noisy shoes, jangling jewelry, gum chewing, knuckle popping, fingernail biting, playing pranks, eating or drinking in front of patients and visitors, avoiding wearing a hearing aid when you need one, interrupting people when they're talking, and smoking in nondesignated areas.

6. Explain how grammar and vocabulary affect your image.

Grammar and vocabulary can negatively affect your image. Examples include using language that annoys or offends other people, such as calling someone "honey," "sweetie," or "dear," or using sexually explicit or racially demeaning terms. Poor grammar is a warning signal, indicating a lack of education and refinement.

7. Describe why is it important to maintain professionalism after hours.

Even after work hours, some of your actions can affect your professional image. You never know when you might run into someone you work with after hours. Your reputation goes with you every place you go. It's OK to "let your hair down" and have a good time, but don't let your guard down, too. Always think before you act.

8. List three examples of personal management skills.

Personal management skills include the ability to manage time, finances, stress, and change. Critical-thinking and problem-solving skills are also examples.

9. Explain why time management skills are important, and list three time management strategies.

You can't create more hours in the day, but you can seize control of the time you have. Time is one of your most precious, and most limited, commodities. Learning how to manage it appropriately can have a huge impact on your personal and professional life. Time management strategies include using a pocket-sized calendar to record appointments, allowing extra time to get from one place to the next, anticipating that things might take longer than you hope, having a contingency plan for when transportation and child-care problems occur, avoiding procrastination, breaking big projects into smaller pieces and tackling one at a time, making lists and ranking items as to priority, learning to say "no," and eliminating activities that waste time.

10. Explain why personal financial management skills are important, and list three financial management strategies.

Personal financial management skills are important because financial problems can have a negative affect on your reputation as a professional. Overspending on credit cards, failing to pay bills on time, and falling behind on loan payments can result in creditors calling you at work as well as other forms of embarrassment. Financial management strategies include keeping your checking account balanced, living within a budget, and avoiding the temptation to buy things on credit. Other strategies include planning ahead for unforeseen expenses, having a savings plan, possessing sufficient insurance, and setting priorities for allocating limited resources.

11. List three examples of how stress can affect someone's health and list three strategies to help manage stress.

Stress can affect your physical, mental, and emotional health and is viewed as a contributing factor to several different diseases and abnormalities. Stress can make you sick and cause headaches, fatigue, sleep problems, diarrhea, indigestion, ulcers, hypertension, dizziness, hives, grinding teeth, skin disorders, and stuttering. Stress has also been linked with heart attacks, high blood pressure, alcoholism, depression, and abuse. Your ability to perform the duties of your job may also be affected by stress. Strategies to help manage stress include being able to recognize when, why, and how stress is affecting you and where the stress is coming from. Better understanding sources and symptoms of stress will help you alleviate it. Find someone you can discuss your stress with and get some professional help when you need it. Try to keep your stress at work from affecting your home life and your relationships with family and friends. Try to keep stress in your personal life from affecting your work. Remember that any change results in stress, even changes that you perceive as good ones. Learn to relax, schedule time for recreation and other personal interests, maintain a healthy balance between work and play, get plenty of sleep, eat properly, and avoid alcohol and drugs. Strengthen interpersonal communication and conflict resolution skills, and don't keep negative feelings bottled up. Know your limits, avoid perfectionism, and feel good about your accomplishments.

12. What is a positive self-image and why is it important?

A positive self-image means feeling good about yourself and possessing high levels of self-esteem and self-respect. Having a positive self-image is important because it helps you manage stress by feeling happy and well adjusted.

13. Why are creative-thinking and problem-solving skills important?

Every day we're faced with a variety of problems to solve, both in our personal lives and at work. By using critical-thinking skills and a systematic approach to addressing problems, you can usually come up with a solution that will work. These skills are mandatory for a well-orchestrated personal and professional life.

14. List the steps involved in problem solving.

The steps involved in problem solving are: (a) identify a problem when you see one, (b) define exactly what the problem is, (c) gather information to learn more about the problem, (d) identify possible solutions, and (e) decide which solution is best.

15. What are adaptive skills and why are they important in today's health care workplace?

Adaptive skills give a person the ability to adjust to change. Years ago, health care workers were encouraged to cope with change. Later, everyone was encouraged to manage change. Today, because things change so rapidly, workers must embrace and lead change. Adaptive skills can help you view change in a positive way and take advantage of the opportunities that result from change.

Chapter Five: Growth and Advancement

1. Describe the difference between a stagnant career and a dynamic career.

A stagnant career is dull, sluggish, and without motion. A dynamic career is energetic, vigorous, and in motion. Health care workers strive for a dynamic career, always looking for opportunities to learn new things, acquire new skills, accept new responsibilities, and grow personally and professionally.

2. What are occupational preferences?

Occupational preferences are the types of work and work settings that an individual prefers.

3. What is job shadowing and how can it help in career exploration?

Job shadowing is when you observe other workers to see what their jobs are like. This is one of the best ways to investigate career options and decide in what direction to head.

4. What are transferable skills and how do they apply in career planning?

Transferable skills are skills acquired in one job that are applicable in another job. Once you've identified your transferable skills, you'll have more insight as to the variety of employment opportunities open to you. In career planning, you might wish to apply your transferable skills in the same occupational field as you work in now or in another field altogether.

5. What are abilities and aptitude?

Abilities are your current knowledge and skills. Aptitude is your capacity to learn more.

6. What are personal assessments and why are they important?

Personal assessments are questionnaires and tests that identify interests and evaluate abilities. Assessments are like insurance policies—they help ensure you're on the right track and adequately prepared to tackle the next step in your career.

7. What are basic skills and why are they important?

Basic skills are fundamental aptitudes in reading, language, and math. Strong basic skills are the foundation upon which you build new knowledge and skills. If your basic skills are weak and you don't shore them up first, you could have difficulty advancing your education.

8. Define *goals, short-term goals,* and *long-term goals,* and explain why goals are important.

Goals are objects or ends that one strives to attain; aims. Short-term goals are those goals attained in a relatively brief period of time—up to about two years. Long-term goals take longer to attain and often involve meeting several short-term goals along the way. Goals are important because they are the stepping-stones that help you progress from where you are now to where you eventually want to be in your career.

9. Describe what is meant by setting "realistic" goals, and explain how a role model and mentor can help you make sure your goals are attainable.

Realistic goals are those that are attainable and "right for you." A role model already has the kind of abilities, education, job, and professional reputation that you aspire to achieve yourself, so you can observe what makes him or her successful and decide if that person's approach would also work for you. Although he or she has not necessarily achieved the same goals you hope to achieve, a mentor can provide you with insight, advice, and encouragement to help you each step of the way.

10. Why should you be a role model and mentor for other people?

We're all "on this road together," and it's important for you to help other people meet their goals, too.

11. What is postsecondary education?

Postsecondary education occurs after you've graduated from high school.

12. Why is it a good idea to take just one college course first?

Taking just one college course first helps you "get your feet wet" prior to applying for an entire educational program. It gives you the opportunity to see what college-level course work is like without having to take several courses at the same time. You'll also get into the habit of studying, taking tests, and completing course assignments on time.

13. What role does risk taking play in career advancement?

Expect to take some risks. This does not mean making decisions in a foolish or haphazard way, but it does mean taking some well-thought-out, calculated steps that force you to stretch a little bit.

14. List three resources that can help you with career advancement.

Resources to help you with career advancement include the library, Internet, career and occupational reference books, educational and career counselors at local schools, human resources consultants at work, and the *It's a Jungle Out There! An Insider's Outlook on Jobs in Health Care* book.

15. What is constructive criticism and how can it help you?

Constructive criticism is viewing one's weaknesses in a way that leads to positive improvement. It's important to learn all you can about the impression you make on others and look for ways to improve. Constructive criticism is geared to make you an even better professional.

16. What is networking and why is it valuable?

Networking is interacting with a variety of people in different settings. Networking is valuable because it helps you strengthen your interpersonal skills and learn more about job opportunities, both within your own organization and in other organizations throughout your community.

17. Discuss the importance of "expecting the unexpected."

It's important to keep your eyes open for other opportunities the might arise when you least expect it. Jobs are being redesigned, departments are being reorganized, and health care services are moving from the hospital setting to outpatient facilities. Increasing numbers of workers are being trained, cross-trained, and retrained for new responsibilities. Unexpected changes can open up new career options.

18. What is a résumé?

A résumé is a document used in applying for a job or for admission into an educational program, describing your background and qualifications.

19. Why is an application form an important part of the selection process?

An application form is an important part of the selection process because it's reviewed closely by employers and admissions committee members to determine if an applicant can read and follow directions. It's also a sample of your written communication skills. Often, employers and program admissions committees screen applicants first to decide which applicants will get interviews and which ones won't. This screening usually involves an evaluation of the application form as well as the applicant's résumé.

20. List three important factors in completing and submitting an application form appropriately.

Make sure the application form gets submitted to the right place on time. Spend an adequate amount of time preparing the application form. Fill it out yourself; don't have someone else do it for you. It's best to type the information but, if handwritten, make sure the writing is legible. Follow the directions, make sure all words are spelled correctly, and list accurate dates for previous work experience and education. Make sure the application form is complete and never falsify any information. If the application form calls for a brief statement on why you're applying for the job or for the program, take some time to think about your answer before writing it. Use your best written communication skills to convince the reviewers that you've thought about the job or the program and you know it's a good match for you, your interests, and your skills.

21. What is preemployment or preadmission testing and why is it done?

Preemployment or preadmission testing is when applicants are given written or practical exams to assess their current skills. Employers and admissions committee members need to know if you're qualified for the job or the program and if you have the knowledge and skills necessary to be successful.

22. What are official transcripts?

Official transcripts are grade reports that are printed, sealed, and mailed directly to the recipient to prevent tampering by the applicant.

23. List five important factors in participating in an interview for a new job or for admission into a training program.

When participating in an interview for a new job or for admission into a training program, it's important to look your best, wear appropriate clothing and accessories, and be well groomed. You should smile, offer a firm handshake, and remember the names of people you're introduced to. Apply your best interpersonal communication skills. Maintain your composure, be confident, and self-assured. Describe the skills and abilities you would bring to the job or to the program. Sit up straight, don't chew gum or bite your fingernails, and try to relax. Concentrate on each question and think before you answer. Put your best critical-thinking and problem-solving skills to work, and answer questions to the best of your ability. It's OK for you to ask questions too, but avoid asking questions that are already answered in whatever printed material may have been made available to you in advance. Give some thought to how you would respond to questions about pay and benefit requirements, just in case those types of questions are asked during your first interview. When applying for admission into an educational program, ask if the program is accredited, investigate all expenses, and inquire about average starting pay and employment opportunities for graduates. Also ask about the students' success rate in the program, what percent of graduates find jobs in the local area, and what percent pass national certification exams on the first attempt. Follow up job interviews or program selection interviews with a short thank-you note.

24. Explain why it's important never to falsify or exaggerate information about yourself on an application form or during an interview.

It's important to stand on your own merits and never falsify or exaggerate any information. Misrepresentation is dishonest and constitutes fraud. It's unprofessional, unethical, and likely to result in your dismissal should your lies ever be discovered.

25. Why is it important to pull together everything you've learned about professionalism during the application, interviewing, and selection process?

Pulling together everything you've learned about professionalism is important during the application, interviewing, and selection process because making a positive first impression is a key step in getting selected for a new job or for admission into an educational program. If you do get selected, you'll be on the road to achieving another goal. If you don't get selected, you'll know you did your best and will have learned something in the process.

Supplemental Learning Resources

It's a Jungle Out There! An Insider's Outlook on Jobs in Health Care

Written for students, teachers, advisers, and parents, this up-to-date booklet describes why and how health care is changing and the impact of change on career and employment opportunities. Discusses organizational restructuring, work redesign, multiskilling, and new roles for health care workers. Topics include the role of teams, skills in demand, and how to prepare for the health care workplace of tomorrow. 1996, by Sherry Makely, Ph.D., RT-R, and Lana Christian, MT, MA, CRC, Pine Ridge Publications, Inc.

Ordering information: Pine Ridge Publications, Inc., 1051 West Burma Road, Bloomington, IN 47404; phone 812-876-7211; fax 812-876-9117; ISBN 0-9652954-0-0.

Multiskilled Health Care Workers: Issues and Approaches to Cross-Training

Written for managers, educators, workers, and students, this book describes the evolution of cross-training and how multiskilled personnel provide team-based care in today's restructured health care organizations. Topics include skill combinations, team composition, and approaches to educating and employing multiskilled personnel. 1998, by Sherry Makely, Ph.D., RT-R, Pine Ridge Publications, Inc.

Ordering information: Pine Ridge Publications, Inc., 1051 West Burma Road, Bloomington, IN, 47404; phone 812-876-7211; fax 812-876-9117; ISBN 0-9652954-3-5.

Index